PREPARING FOR CONTACT

A Metamorphosis of Consciousness

by

Lyssa Royal and Keith Priest

A Royal Priest Research Book

Published by:
Royal Priest Research Press
c/o PO Box 30973
Phoenix, Arizona 85046

Cover Art:
Corey Wolfe
18612 N.E. Risto Rd.
Battleground, Washington 98602

First Printing, February 1994

Publisher's Cataloging in Publication
(Prepared by Quality Books Inc.)

Royal, Lyssa.
    Preparing for contact : a metamorphosis of consciousness / by Lyssa Royal and Keith Priest.
    p. cm.
    ISBN 0-9631320-2-4

    1. Spirit writings. 2. Unidentified flying objects--
Miscellanea. 3. Life on other planets--Forecasting--Miscellanea
4. New Age movement--Miscellanea. I. Priest, Keith. II. Title.

BF1311.S45R69 1994   133.9'3
                                       QBI93-22376

Dedication

To all of you star children with your feet on the ground and your head in the stars. Thank you for holding the dream.

Table of Contents

Introduction
by Lyssa Royal

This book is a combination of narrative, channeled material, and personal experiences. Many individuals distrust, dislike, or fear channeled material and may judge it prematurely. We ask that you read it not because it *is* or it *isn't* channeled. Read it because the material presents an alternate point of view. Our sources never claim they have *the* truth. They claim they have information that is meant to be taken as information only — data to be added to the collective human understanding.

I have provided all the channeled material in this book and it is edited only for grammatical and structural reasons. The transcripts are taken from either public or private sessions. The sources of the channeled material are described below.

I began channeling in 1985 and was trained formally by a highly respected channel in Los Angeles. My channeling process has been unique in that I have been committed to pushing my abilities to their limits — into realms perhaps as yet unexplored. It is because of my willingness to enter these unexplored realms that some of this information has been obtained. I will say that I am my own worst critic! Because of this, I tend to push myself to channel the answers to some of my most profound questions. In 1986 I began the deliberate choice of developing my channeling ability in order to access the quality and depth of information that is presented in our books, *The Prism of Lyra*, *Visitors from Within*, and now *Preparing for Contact*.

The channeling process is simple. I put myself into a meditative state in which my personality disconnects from my normal perception of reality. Another consciousness (or entity) links energetically and telepathically with my brain and then uses it as a translation device for the concepts discussed. In no way am I "taken over" by another entity. It is entirely a cooperative process between myself and the entity. It can be discontinued at any time by my choice. When the session is completed, I retain only a dreamlike memory of what has transpired.

While in trance, the entities through me are questioned by co-author Keith Priest and/or various other individuals attending the private or public gathering. The audience questions are presented in italics and the channeled responses are in normal text.

In no way is it necessary for the reader to believe the entities are who they say they are. It is also unnecessary for the information to be accepted verbatim. Some will agree with the information presented and some will disagree. The presentation of *all* facets of the subject matter is necessary for a coherent and complete understanding of the whole picture.

There are several entities who are channeled for our research. Three of those entities have provided the material for this book. We describe them below because they each have different personalities that will be reflected in the way they present their material.

Sasha claims to be a physical female from the Pleiades. She is about five feet tall with light-brown shoulder-length hair and large, light-brown, almond-shaped eyes. She calls herself a cultural engineer and psycho-sociologist, specializing in opening contact with planets who are ready to enter the galactic community. She has had contact with other extraterrestrial races as well as our own, and provides much information about the relationship between different species and the evolutionary patterns of developing planets. Because of this, Sasha has channeled the majority of the information in *Preparing for Contact*.

Bashar claims to be a physical male extraterrestrial from the Essassani species. The name "Bashar" is a word that has several meanings: "The man" (Arabic), "the messenger" (Armenian), and "commander" (Arabic). He chose that name to reflect several facets of his personality. The Essassani species can also be described as a hybrid species resulting from the genetic cross between the Earth human and the Zeta Reticuli visitors. Bashar is channeled by only a few people on Earth and infrequently speaks through Lyssa. (His primary channel is Darryl Anka.) Bashar provided only a portion of one chapter for this book.

Germane considers himself to be a nonphysical group consciousness. He claims that he represents a future integrated version of the galactic family of which we on Earth are a part. He often channels about extraterrestrial history, and he was responsible for a large portion of the information in Royal Priest Research's first book, *The Prism of Lyra*. He chose the name Germane because in English it means "coming from the same source." There is no connection with St. Germain. The term "he" is used in reference to Germane for convenience only. Germane is actually a group, and refers to itself as "we." In this book, Germane provides only a portion of one chapter.

Again, it is not necessary to believe in the origin of this material for the reader to benefit from it. Use the material presented to stimulate your own search for truth. I have often been asked if I really believe that I channel extraterrestrial entities. I have answered that it is not a matter of belief or disbelief. Instead, the importance lies in where the information and the channeling process takes me in my understanding. At times I do question the origin of the material, but ultimately I feel that healthy skepticism actually sharpens my skills as a channel.

All I can say is that Sasha, Bashar, and Germane *seem* very real to me. (Actually, I can relate more to Sasha and Bashar because they have physical bodies.) Sasha is as real as any of my human friends even though I have never met her physically (as far as I can remember consciously). The more I channel her, the more real she becomes. If she is simply the product of some undiscovered ability within the human consciousness, then I still consider my relationship with her to be a gift. She has opened doors to the universe for me and I have not ever had to leave my own back yard!

I hope that *Preparing for Contact* will excite you and inspire you to discover your own personal relationship with the extraterrestrial contact phenomenon.

— Lyssa Royal

Preface

In the film *Free Willy*, an orca responds profoundly — and intelligently — to the sounds of a lone harmonica played by a young boy. Was it sound which drew the orca to the boy? Or was it perhaps the boy's emotions? Something sparked a strong, almost telepathic connection between these two different species — cetacean and human.

Free Willy is just a film. Yet there are hundreds of stories of interspecies communication as profound between man and dolphin or whale.

In the mid-1980s the author Lyssa Royal and several friends went to the marine park Sea World in San Diego, California. Their interest was in making contact — any contact — between themselves and the park's cetaceans (dolphins and whales). The experiences they had were profound indeed.

Seven of them stood together at the dolphin petting pool. In the pool were pilot whales and several species of dolphins all being fed and kept busy by many children and adults. Spontaneously, the group stood together and began to emit a single vocal tone. As each person joined in, the sound reverberated around the tank. The toning was a purely spontaneous act in the moment. All dolphin petting stopped. Slowly, all the bottle-nosed dolphins grouped together and came directly to the group of humans.

As this happened, the human group began to feel an overwhelming sense of joy. These bottle-nosed dolphins then, in unison, bobbed their heads and chests out of the water right in front of the humans. The group kept toning. The dolphins closed their eyes and, with a look of utter serenity, basked in the sounds the humans were making. The dolphins' bellies turned bright pink in their excitement. The humans were crying tears of joy in theirs. After the experience reached its peak, the toning stopped and the dolphins made eye contact with the humans. Then they returned to being fed fish by the tourists.

This experience changed the human group that day. In their exuberance, they proceeded to the huge orca tank that housed two orcas at the time. They were swimming around with disinterest, ignoring the few people who pounded on the tank.

The group of seven humans stood in a secluded location at one of the tanks. Still buoyed by the excitement of the dolphin encounter, they began to emit a tone vocally directly to the plexiglass of the orca tank. Several minutes later the group began to hear whalesong. The urge was to stop toning in order to hear the beautiful music, but instead they kept toning.

To their amazement, they saw the massive body of an orca approach. He stopped directly in front of the group on the other side of the plexiglass and began singing. The orca made direct eye contact with the group as both sang together. The emotion was so overwhelming that tears began flowing. The humans placed their hands upon the tank and the orca drew closer — still maintaining eye contact. His songs felt like piercing waves of ecstasy. Eventually the singing and toning stopped. The humans returned to being human, and the orca returned to being an orca. But for those few brief minutes, they *connected*.

Many are aware of the belief that cetaceans are not just "smart fish," but another sentient life form on Earth which we have overlooked because of their obvious difference to humans. If this is in fact true, then we have an "alien" life form here in our very seas with which to practice communication skills before we reach for the stars.

It is a very romantic fantasy to believe that what awaits us in space is a *Star Trek* universe — where everyone speaks Standard (English) and communication is relatively easy. Though *Star Trek* has no doubt played one of the most significant fictional roles in preparing us for the future, we still have a long way to go. We must learn to recognize alien sentience when it does not come in the humanoid package. We must also learn to be creative in our methods of communication. And most of all, we must learn the secrets of human consciousness and strive to transform ourselves beyond our perceived limitations. We must trust in humankind enough to plunge into the worlds of the unconscious, the spiritual, and the unknown. For it is here that many answers await our discovery.

In this book we will begin the plunge by exploring such subjects as the human ego, consciousness, and memory — all of which tremendously affect the extraterrestrial contact experience. We will also explore the consciousness and reality paradigm of the extraterrestrials in order to gain a perspective that will prepare us for the challenges of ET contact. But most of all, we will explore the creation of a common ground – a "place" where humans and extraterrestrials can meet on equal footing to begin the next phase of human evolution.

There are so many aspects to the extraterrestrial contact experience that they could fill at least five volumes. Since we had to condense our exploration into one book, we have chosen the aspect of the phenomenon which excites us the most: How the human psyche responds to the extraterrestrial presence. We know little about this subject and have few tools with which to measure the phenomenon, because it often defies physical reality itself. We will not be discussing Unidentified Flying Objects (UFOs), abductions, or crashed saucers. Instead, we will explore the inner landscape of humans as they open themselves to contact with extraterrestrial beings.

To some, this information may seem a bit esoteric. It is not intended to be. We simply know no other way of communicating these ideas because the subject matter itself is so elusive and intangible. This book is not so much analytical as it is experiential – attempting to stimulate rather than indoctrinate – reflecting our belief that the key to comprehending the phenomenon is by adding spirit and imagination to the intellect.

So often an investigation of a sighting or encounter ignores the human part of the experience. How does the experience affect the observer? How does the observer interpret the experience on deeper levels of his psyche, and can this lead us to a greater understanding of the contact phenomenon? Can we begin to see this phenomenon through the experience of the observer without denying that there also may be an objective experience on the part of the extraterrestrial?

The ET encounter can be seen as a koan. According to Zen Buddhist terminology, a koan is a puzzle that does not necessarily have an answer. Like a koan, the UFO/ET phenomenon offers the opportunity to deprogram the mind, making enlightenment possible. But the UFO/ET is not the complete koan itself. We *and* the ETs are the koan—we come together as one fluid idea or mandala. And as soon as we approach an answer, the question changes! At that point the same paradigm no longer exists in which to frame the original question.

The ET contact experience and related encounters are koans that lead us to another level of awareness within ourselves. This concept of layers upon layers of new awareness (which is often triggered by a koan) is what we wish to explore with you. Yes, these craft are seen visually and are often just what they appear to be: interplanetary/interdimensional craft piloted by sentient beings—sometimes very similar to ourselves—with their own agendas and their own way of viewing reality. Yet that does not negate the fact that the primary effect of contact is a transformative one for the observer, and sometimes a disturbing one at that.

We are not so much looking for proof of ET contact, but for the footprints of contact—footprints on the surface of the human psyche. Metaphysical forensics, if you will. If we can uncover when contact has occurred, how the human psyche processes the information, and how the experience is interpreted, then maybe we can get some idea about where these footprints lead.

Contact is not just about a ship landing and an ET getting out to shake hands with us. Neither is contact about being dragged from a warm bed in the middle of the night and experiencing a medical examination. Contact is nothing short of two separate species forming a holographic meeting ground and beginning to dream the same dream. Contact represents the next step in human evolution.

Most of the material on the following pages is channeled by an entity (Sasha) who claims to be a physical female extraterrestrial from a planet in the Pleiades colonies. According to Sasha, there are approximately 250 populated worlds (most of which orbit stars we cannot yet see in the vicinity of the Pleiades) that are part of her Pleiadian neighborbood. For our convenience, she has given her planet a name to which we may refer in English—"Mandala." Even though she spends much of her professional career in studies and operations with various species who are members of the Association of Worlds, she still experiences her own bias, which is a product of her species history and personal perspective.

Sasha's material has a Pleiadian flavor. The information she shares about the contact experience comes from a Pleiadian point of view. For the most part, she does not address contact with lesser-evolved species who are closer to humans on the evolutionary scale. She instead focuses on the more evolved ETs who are genetic relatives of humanity (Pleiadians, Essassani, Future Earth, and others) and how their contacts impact human consciousness. From our point of view, the information and beliefs presented here by Sasha, Bashar, and Germane are widely held by the ET groups with which we frequently work in our research.

There are certain ideas in ufology that are commonly avoided by most researchers. These neglected areas have to do with the contactees themselves. It is ironic that ufology spends so much brain power on analyzing photos, arguing over data, and writing reports. Meanwhile, the one person truly touched by the encounter (the observer) is either ignored, discredited, or subjected to intense scrutiny. This observer, unbeknownst to the ufologist, may embody some of the most astounding discoveries in human consciousness ever made! It is these observers/contactees who are forever changed. It is these contactees who, by their singular footprints into the jungle of the unknown, may be forging a path that humanity may someday be required to follow.

We are entering an age now where we no longer need to be victims of extraterrestrial contact for it to enter our reality and be validated by the masses. This coming age requires us to be *participants* of contact. This is a phenomenon that will enter the life of every human at some point in the future. It cannot be denied. It cannot be ignored. And it certainly cannot be put off forever. The day will come when we must accept and acknowledge our own evolution by entering species adulthood and becoming responsible galactic neighbors. The only way we can transcend the stigma of being "victims" of ET contact is by willingly initiating it.

Contact with newly discovered races and tribes has been part of our Earth's history and a significant part of our own societal evolution. So it is that contact with extraterrestrial species is part of a planet's global evolution. By willingly engaging the extraterrestrials in open contact, we as a planetary species send out a beacon to the universe proclaiming our rite of passage — our coming of age into a galactic community of which we have always been a part but are now beginning to consciously recognize.

Humanity is witnessing its own birth. The labor pains felt today represent the achievements of tomorrow. The ET contact experience is not the cause of this transformation; it is a symptom of it. Yet during this profound transformation we need guidance as we grope around in the dark. We've reached a point now where the guidance cannot come from a source outside of ourselves. Because of this, we must explore our inner landscape — the places where we hide experiences that don't conform to our rigid view of reality. It is here amongst the archetypes, repressed memories, and inner fears where we will find our answers about ourselves and how we fit within the universal landscape.

Quantum physics has been exploring the idea that the observer and the observed are part of the same one thing. We do not exist within a random, unconnected universe, but within a rich tapestry where all pieces are interwoven together. The ETs, their ships, the contactees, and even the ufologists are all part of a grand dance. In the following pages we will all learn some new steps to this dance together. But remember one thing: The music never stops, and the dance is eternal.

1

Preparing for Contact

For so long we have viewed extraterrestrial contact as something that happens *to* us. We have often wondered why some people seem to receive contact while others continue to stare curiously at an empty sky. Could it be possible that we have within our power the ability to take some forward steps toward a common meeting ground with extraterrestrials? If so, what do we have to do as individuals to prepare for the experience of coming face to face with an extraterrestrial?

As this book was being researched, one thing became clear: The ways we have been imagining the ideal contact experience is actually limiting the experience itself. We need a whole new understanding about ET contact (and the human consciousness) that will allow us to break through our rigid beliefs about the validity of that contact.

In this chapter, Germane begins by addressing the contact issue as a vehicle for personal growth. Germane's ideas are for the sole purpose of expanding the boundaries and perceived limitations of our consciousness even further than we thought possible. Sasha concludes the chapter by addressing some of the most commonly asked questions about ET contact.

Δ Δ Δ

Germane: Let us begin by discussing the idea of preparing for extraterrestrial contact. We are going to begin by saying this: There is no magic key. There is no magic pill that you can take. There is no magic incantation that is going to bring about contact. The only thing that will bring about the contact you desire is your own personal growth and your own personal processing so that your view of reality will change. Once your view of reality changes, the contact that you seek will be there.

We do not mean that when your view of reality changes you will draw contact to you. No. *Contact is already going on.* It has been going on with humans since before recorded history. What we mean by the above statement is that when your view of reality changes, when your perceptions change, you will then be able to see what has been there all along.

One of the things we are going to address in this book is the compartmentalization of the human consciousness that allows for your unawareness of the contact already happening. We would first like to talk about seven major ideas. Please know that these are not magic keys. Rather, these seven points are going to help you change your perceptions of reality so that you will then be able to begin perceiving the contact that has existed all along. These are by no means the only things you can do. But they are a good start. This will help you begin integrating your consciousness and learn to perceive in a very different way.

1. Acknowledge Inevitability. Most of you have no problem with this. Within your deepest self, acknowledge the reality and the inevitability of an open relationship with beings not of your realm. When we say, "acknowledge inevitability," we are not necessarily talking about your conscious, logical minds. We are talking about an emotional shift. It is a shift that defies verbal description. It is a shift within you where an emotional certainty exists about the inevitability of contact. This is not a *hope* for contact. Hope implies that there is doubt, however small. We are instead talking about a complete certainty on an emotional level about contact. This goes far beyond the intellectual level.

If any of you are sitting there thinking, "Yes, I emotionally acknowledge the inevitability of contact," we are going to say that is wonderful. However, there are compartmentalized portions of the human consciousness that fear, disbelieve, and judge well beyond what the

2

conscious mind is aware of.

So, for the sake of this exercise, pretend that none of you have achieved this. (Sorry if this hurts your ego! This exercise will actually help you in the long run.) It is important that you give yourself permission to play and pretend here. The consciousnesses of some of the ETs and other beings (such as the cetaceans) are very playful. To get to the common ground where you can communicate together, you must also be able to play.

Go within yourself. Imagine a part of you that is not acknowledging the inevitability of contact. What does it look like? Again, you don't have to think really hard for the answer. *Feel* an answer. Put the question out to the universe and see what happens. Your answer might take the following shape: Is there a fear or dread inside of you that says contact *won't* happen? If there is, that is an indication that you have not, on the emotional level, acknowledged the inevitability. Fear is always a wonderful signpost.

2. Personal Truth versus Disinformation. As you know in your UFO research circles, there are many opinions about UFOs and related subjects. Those of you who are researching get a bit confused because of all these opinions. However, the only opinion that really counts is the one that you hold. The one that you hold is going to dictate how contact happens for you. So, start first on the intellectual level.

On the intellectual level, start throwing away all of the ideas that you think are poppycock. Get to the root of what your conscious mind believes about contact. After you've done your intellectual homework, we're going to ask you to do your emotional homework. Go within and ask yourself the following question: "Is there anything that I fear about ET contact?" Do you fear that you could be abducted and mutilated? Or do you fear that you are going to be eaten by ETs? The most common fear existing deep within is that in the face of contact, the human will lose his or her ego. This fear is something that the conscious mind cannot always access because the conscious mind is ruled by the ego. This is why your intellect is going to to be of little help to you in examining your inner beliefs.

Go within. Be blatantly honest with yourself. The most common fear for humanity right now that cannot be accessed by the intellect is the fear of the loss of your ego. Let us describe what we mean by this, using a simplistic illustration. You are sitting in your house. Suddenly, there is a bright light in the back yard and a blue light shines through the window. You get an adrenalin rush. You hear footsteps going toward the back door. Knock, knock. You go to the door and open it. You stand face to face with a Pleiadian.

Many of you reading this might think, "That is so exciting. I would embrace them and invite them in." But a lot more happens on levels deeper than the conscious interaction. When you open the door and you look at that alien, one thing has to happen. There must be an energetic bridge between you that forms the common ground upon which you can communicate. This means that your vibration must suddenly accelerate very quickly. When that happens, the ego becomes frightened and breaks off the contact. If you've trained yourself through time with dreamstate ET interactions, then it is not going to be as traumatic. This is one of the reasons why your dreamstate contact happens. It is an acclimation to the ET energy.

This is what we mean by going deep within and looking for your own truth and your own secret fears about this contact phenomenon. If you can access them emotionally, you are going to accelerate your growth toward a more easy contact rather than something that panics the ego.

3. Embrace Humanity. This one is pretty obvious. How can humans embrace open contact, when you can't even embrace each other? How can you accept an open and equal relationship of respect with the Pleiadians, for instance, if you cannot do so with those of other races or sexual preferences on Earth? Contact cannot happen in its fullest form until humanity embraces itself. We are talking about both the conscious and the unconscious levels.

On the conscious level, many of you are saying to yourselves, "Yes, I accept the equality of all people." But on a deep emotional level, how many of you are willing to embrace someone even when they frighten you? Now, we are not asking you to run out and embrace a serial killer. All we are asking you to do is to examine the unconscious part of you that refuses to embrace the people you fear. Examine that. Go within. Whom do you fear in your own society? Pick them out and look at what they represent for you as individuals. That is going to be a key toward moving you through the fears that

4

keep all of you separated from each other, and keep your species separated from your ET forefathers.

This is a very, very powerful step. If your intellect ever tells you that you have done all your homework for this, you have not. But don't worry about completing this step. This is not about completion. The goal of this process is not as important as the process itself. You are always going to be able to accept and love more. This is not a finite idea. If you try to get to the finish line, you will find there really isn't a finish line. Just seek more.

Go within and seek those you fear. Learn from that knowledge. Then begin to learn what that person represents within you. Then learn to embrace that within yourself. As this is done, your reality begins to change. Your world begins to change. Your relationship to the ETs begins to change.

You have all heard that you create your reality from inside. Actually, everything you see is a projection of your inner world. Seek to *feel* (not *know*) the connection that you have with the reality around you. Recognize that the person sitting next to you right now, whether you know them or not, is your creation. This doesn't mean that they do not exist outside of you. You simply create your *version* of them with which to interact.

4. Interspecies Communication. This is probably one of the easiest steps. You have many alien species on Earth, and all of them have a certain type of sentience. It's not the same type of sentience that you have, but it is still sentience. As you learn to communicate with these different species, you are going to begin shifting your perception of reality so that reality itself will change.

When we suggest that you learn to communicate with these other species, we are not talking about communicating according to *your* rules of communication. This doesn't mean sticking a dolphin in an aquarium and teaching him how to communicate in sign language. Those are *your* rules of language. Instead, reach out into *their* realm. You don't have to play exclusively by their rules, either. Find a common ground. We guarantee that if you are willing to reach toward the common ground, they will do the same thing. If you expect consciousness to communicate with you by your rules, you will always be disappointed. They don't know what your rules are!

Your rules might be plain to you, but not to those with whom you are trying to communicate. This is the difficulty with the SETI program. You are blasting radio waves into space and searching for alien radio transmissions, expecting the aliens to communicate according to *your* rules of communication. That is like sending smoke signals to NASA, expecting a return communication! But it is part of the whole process of learning and growing. It is a very positive step for your species. Those of you who are visionaries can nudge it along a little further by learning to enter the common ground and communicate there.

Those of you who have had communication with ETs in your dreams have found a way to enter this common ground through the dream state. In the dream state, the ETs are not communicating with you according to your rules. But they are not communicating according to their rules, either. The dream state is the common ground in this instance. Then when humans wake up, they get frustrated because they cannot remember. They say, "Damn those ETs! Why can't they communicate with me when I am awake, so it can mean something!" The lesson here is to learn to understand the language of the common ground.

5. Confront Your Fears. Humans fear certain things. You may be afraid of snakes or small spaces, for example. The fears we are talking about are not those. We are talking about fears of which your conscious mind is unaware. We are talking about fears that your unconscious mind is living with. Your conscious mind/ego protects you from knowing about these fears. These are the ones we are talking about.

Again, it is tempting to get caught up analyzing this with the intellect. Your intellect represents your conscious mind (ego) and therefore cannot communicate to you what the unconscious is fearing. So in order to deal with these deep, deep inner fears, you will need to do work on other levels. Each of you can find your own tools. However, some examples are: rebirthing, regression, or anything that uses archetypes, such as dream work or certain types of Native American ritual. Do whatever you can to unlock the unconscious. The changes you will experience can be profound. Some of you may experience a tremendous amount of freedom. Some of you may experience a period of great turmoil. Do not assume that turmoil, if

6

it happens, is negative. It is not. The unconscious is like Pandora's box. When you open the lid on the unconscious, much of the scary stuff comes out before it balances itself out.

So what does this have to do with preparing for contact? Let us give you an illustration. Imagine the body of a woman who is speaking to you. Assume that her head is her conscious mind. The area from her neck to her hips represents her subconscious; from her hips to her feet is the unconscious. Those of you in the audience sitting in the back of a room can see her only from the chest up. It is easy to assume that the only thing that is important is her head. From that vantage point, the only thing giving you anything of value that you can estimate is her head. Therefore, her head must be ruling this interaction.

This is the way you look at each other. When you talk to your friends, your egos (that is, your heads) talk to each other. What about the rest of you — the subconscious and the unconscious? Do they talk to each other also, unbeknownst to the head/ego? Yes!

When an ET comes into a room, for example, this ET sees the speaker's *whole body*, not just the head/ego. The ET recognizes that the body is a holistic unit. It is not just a talking head, but part of a system. This is what we mean by compartmentalization.

When those listening to a speaker from the back of a room can see only the speaker's head, you assume that the head is the only thing that counts. You compartmentalize. The head (ego), torso (subconscious), and legs (unconscious) are believed to be separate things that do not have a relationship with each other. You learn how to live with this compartmentalization. When an ET communicates with you, your *entire being* (using the analogy of your legs, torso, and head) hears the communication. Each compartment processes the information differently. But because you've fooled yourself into believing that the only thing which matters is the head/ego, you believe the communication is invalid if the dominant receiver of the communication is not your head/ego. The message you put out is, "Don't communicate with me if my head/ego can't hear it!"

The ET, however, does not understand compartmentalization. He will communicate with you on whatever level he can, which, as you will see later, is usually on the subconscious level. He cannot under-

7

stand why you can't hear him within your total being and why you are not responding. You are not responding because the part of you actually hearing the communication (torso/subconscious or legs/unconscious) cannot answer back using the language of the head/ego. So your head/ego doesn't perceive the interaction at all. That's what happens when consciousness is compartmentalized. It is not that the ETs are ignoring you. It is just that the torso/subconscious and legs/unconscious are hearing the communication, but the only part of you that can respond in this reality and pass information to the intellect is the head/ego! And all along the head/ego is saying, "Well, there aren't any ETs, because I'm not hearing any contact!"

It may seem like we've strayed from the issue of confronting your fears. However, your fears are lodged in the compartmentalized parts of you, and it is fear that *keeps* you compartmentalized. This is a very logical and orderly way of keeping you safe. It is a defense mechanism and has worked quite well for you. So ask yourself the following question: "What is more important? To stay compartmentalized and give my ego the illusion of safety, or learn to decompartmentalize myself and integrate as a whole being?" In order to do that you'll have to confront your fears. Once they are confronted, the ETs can talk to you as a whole being. You can then answer back as a whole being as well.

So, it is up to each of you to choose what you want to do. That is why confronting fears is on this list. If you don't do that, it is going to be *very* difficult to integrate your levels of consciousness.

6. Integrate Self and Decompartmentalize. We have told you above how this fits into the process of preparing for contact. If you seek to validate all the levels of your being and to express and receive through all aspects of your being (in combination with confronting your fears), the integration process will be very rapid. As this happens, your perception of reality will begin to change. Let us continue the analogy.

You are sitting in the back row watching the speaker. Earlier, you could see only her head, but now she stands on a chair. You can now see her hands, which express what she is saying. You realize that her legs are moving her head across the room. Earlier you did not think about why her head moved across the room, but now it becomes clear that there are other parts of her, previously ignored, which are part

8

of her communication to you. Now you can see that the head is attached to a body. The head cannot operate without the other compartments. The system works as a holistic unit.

The most important thing that will happen as you prepare for contact is the change in your perception. When that changes, your experiences change. As you can begin imagining from the head down (as in the analogy), so will you then learn integration and decompartmentalization. You will then view reality in an entirely different way. You will begin accepting all forms of communication no matter on what level they are received. And, most importantly, you will become more confident entering the common ground between you.

7. Reclaim Your Power. You have heard this term in many self-help groups. What does it really mean in a functional way? Basically speaking, you have given power to others to tell you what reality is. For instance, you as a people have allowed your authority figures to convince many of you that flying saucers and ETs do not exist. This type of trust in external validation causes separation between your peoples.

When we are talking about power, we are also talking about the entire UFO situation as well. If all of you involved in ufology got together (instead of bickering), confronted those you've allowed to hold your truth and demanded your power back, it would return. You've not yet gotten to the point on that internal level where you've felt you could truly make a difference. This is because you've not acknowledged that you are responsible for the secrecy in the first place. You cannot be a victim and feel your power at the same time. To claim your power fully, you will have to *act* to create the reality you prefer.

What does this mean, then? As a group, all of you who believe firmly in the existence of ETs must begin acting like they already exist. Stop fighting each other. Start living a reality that truly reflects your beliefs. Those of you interested in UFOs are not asking whether they exist. You *know* they exist, so start acting like it! That mass thought will create a mass change of action, which will then change the reality itself. This is much more powerful than you realize.

What does this mean on a personal level? It means that taking your power back is the culmination of these seven steps. The key element

9

of reclaiming your personal power is confronting your fears. You've given your power to your fears and they become bigger than you. They then keep you from acting. As you work with and confront your fears, you automatically begin taking your power back.

These steps are not linear; you don't have to start with step one and finish it before you go to step two. This is a fourth-dimensional model. Whichever step you are able to do in the moment, do it. Or whichever step you are excited about taking, take it. Don't worry about the order or whether you've completed one before you go to the next. They happen simultaneously. What you will find is that you will move through the steps and then start all over again on a new level. You will go through the steps in cycles and rise to higher and higher levels of your own growth.

Δ   Δ   Δ

Sasha: A man once told us a story that we would like to relay to you. This man was doing some inner child and grief work. One night he listened to some drumming music, grieving, and began drumming along with the music. It was sunset. He was drumming, crying, grieving, and feeling a wealth of emotions. He looked up and saw a bright object in the sky above some trees, but didn't pay much attention to it. When he looked up again, he saw three vertical lights adjacent to the first one. He continued to drum and cry, becoming caught in the passion of the moment. As the emotion subsided, he noticed that the three lights were no longer visible together; only one remained. When the tape ended and he stopped his drumming, he noticed that the last light had disappeared.

We love this story because it illustrates something that we feel is very important regarding the subject of ET contact. The lights that he saw were ships. It is not necessarily that they came *to him* while he was drumming; rather, the energy that he generated while he was drumming, grieving and allowing emotion to run through him shifted his reality in such a way that he was able to see the ships that would have been there in any case. There are several keys here we would like to point out that made this experience so profound.

First, he was deep within his emotions, grieving and crying and feeling. He was there in the moment. Passion was flowing through his entire being. Germane spoke about the compartments into which

10

the human consciousness is divided. What this man did while he was drumming and grieving was open a door through those different compartments so they could begin to blend together. Once they blended, his perceptions of reality had to change. He was there in the moment, not in the past or future. He was channeling a tremendous amount of energy through the compartments to bring about a form of integration.

Another aspect is the drumming itself. Germane talked about the value of Native American techniques in allowing you to enter a different state of consciousness. Drumming is one of those techniques. You don't have to rush out and buy some drums! There are other techniques that work as well. For this man, drumming was a link to the primal self. It allowed the other parts of the man's being to relax their defenses. The man could then open up and experience a form of decompartmentalization. This is an example of processing without the head—not putting the head aside, but simply not letting the head rule. This is how the man could have been seen as a whole person by the ETs while they were in their ships. This is why he, as a whole person, could see them. He broke through his barriers. If he had not been drumming and just walked out onto his porch, it would have been much more unlikely that he would have seen them. They would have been there, but he would not have seen them. More and more of these experiences will begin happening.

One of our favorite examples is about the Australian Aborigines. The Aborigines have more open contact as a people than any other group on your planet. This is because of their ability to enter what they call the dreamtime. The Western definition of dreamtime is the time you go to sleep. It is seen as a separate compartment, so to speak. Therefore, in waking time it is very difficult to access dreamtime memories in the Western world. This is because of the way you have compartmentalized your consciousness. However, Aborigines slip into and out of dreamtime and waking time quite easily. They have an ability to cross the veil. They allow the veils to be very thin. The experiences that happen in dreamtime and those that happen in waking time are equally valid and real for them. It is a different cultural conditioning.

We are certainly not asking you to get rid of your Western conditioning. But it would be very beneficial for you to begin to balance

11

your Western conditioning with some of the philosophies of the indigenous cultures. You will find that this will balance you in such a way that you will feel these levels opening up.

We'd like to tell you another story. Some of you have heard this before. The Earth explorer Magellan visited a remote island populated by native people. He anchored his big masted ship out at sea and came to the island with his men in small boats. When they arrived, the natives met them. Even though they saw the men rowing toward shore in the small boats, they couldn't see where those boats came from. It looked as if the boats came from nowhere.

Magellan tried to explain that he came from a large masted ship that was anchored offshore. The natives could not see this ship. The reason for this was that in their reality construct, they had no previous information that would allow for that type of object in their reality. They could allow for the rowboats because they looked like their own canoes, but the masted ship did not fit into their view of reality.

Magellan's men talked to the shamans of this society. Through work with the imagination and through repeated description of the sailing ship, the shamans were eventually able to see it anchored out at sea. On the day they could begin seeing the ship, it was as if a blindfold had been removed. They were astounded. Then the shamans' responsibility was to translate the information about this ship to the natives. The concepts for this ship anchored at sea had to be given to the villagers through several people repeatedly through time before the entire population could see it.

A similar thing is occurring today. If you look at your society as a whole, most of the imaginings of ET contact come from a place of unreality rather than reality. Once the collective vision of your people holds the concept of ET contact, you will then see the contact that has been there all along. Without question, *this will happen!* This is another reason why we recommend some shamanic rituals and Native American practices. It will help your view of reality become more elastic, and you will be able to perceive what has already been there and what is yet to come.

It is difficult to describe this with words, because we are asking you to see something that you can't yet see. So we communicate in the best way we can through the use of analogy. Without question, your ability to have contact will be equal to your ability to perceive an elastic reality. The shamanic teachings will help you to do that, along with the steps that Germane gave you. The goal is to go beyond the known and into the unknown. Automatically assume that you cannot see everything right now.

If this is the case, then why does a farmer in the middle of nowhere with fundamentalist beliefs have contact with UFOs? Is his view of reality elastic enough for this type of contact?

This is a very good question. We are not making a one-on-one correlation. For instance, we are not saying that if Joe has an elastic view of reality he will have contact, and if Mary doesn't, she won't have contact. The greater the number of individuals who are elastic in their beliefs, the more the collective whole will be affected and become more elastic. So someone with a rigid view of reality doesn't have to believe it to see it. He is seeing it, but humanity isn't. In the broader perspective, he is seeing it in *service* to humanity.

Let us give you an example. (Please do not take this literally.) If 60% of the people on Earth had an elastic view of reality, the critical mass created would shift the collective point of view so that your ability to create contact as a whole would be affected. (We are not able to give you an exact percentage that would represent critical mass, because it is not a matter of *quantity*, but of *quality* of energy.) The rural farmer saw the UFO for his own reasons and for his own growth. On another level, he experienced this in service to humanity to help encourage the elastic view of reality. The more elastic that each of you become in your perceptions, the more energy you add to the collective whole's ability to perceive elastic realities. That will eventually trigger mass change in perception.

When do you see that happening?

Well, when do you feel like creating it? It can happen tomorrow, or it can happen within twenty-five years. The next twenty-five years hold the strongest potential for this change in the perception of reality. We read the currents of probable reality and they change from moment to moment.

There is a momentum building in your mass consciousness now. Once that momentum is strong enough to create total change, that will be when the perception shifts. This does not necessarily mean

13

that everyone on your planet will believe in UFOs. That is not what we are talking about. It may not ever manifest like that. Instead, it will be a subtle shift in the human perception of reality. It may not have to do with UFOs at all. But when your perception of reality shifts, extraterrestrial visitations will become a natural part of your reality. It won't be something alien or frightening.

Most of you know about the hundredth-monkey effect. On an island, a process was introduced to some monkeys. As it was used by more and more monkeys, it was eventually picked up spontaneously by a group of monkeys on a faraway island. That is an example of the passing of information through the morphogenetic field, or the non-physical relay station connecting all consciousness. This process happens for humans as well; it will play a major role in helping your mass consciousness to begin perceiving reality differently enough to accept the idea of ET contact. You cannot gauge this through your conscious mind, because this does not occur in the conscious realm.

Regarding the ETs who are already here, what is in it for them? Why are they here?

There are so many species who are connected to Earth that there is not one goal for all of them. There are some common goals, however. One is karmic. There are many ETs who feel that they have wrongly interacted with humans in the past, for instance, by allowing themselves to be worshiped as gods. So they are here attempting to right a wrong they feel they've done.

Another motivation is pure good neighborliness. They want to extend their hands to someone who is going to be entering the galactic community. They are bringing you the proverbial potluck dinner as you enter the neighborhood. They have the plate in their hands and have been ringing the doorbell. They see the lights are on, but no one is home! (We could not resist that one!)

There are many different reasons. As for negative reasons, every once in a while we get some renegade groups who have their own agendas. Please know that in our perception, those renegade groups are a lot fewer than they would have you believe. There are very few.

We recognize you as being part of us. Just like all of you on Earth are one people, all of us in the cosmos are one people. Something that we really like to do is to prepare you to enter space. It is that simple. There are a lot of things for which you will need to be prepared. This is one of the reasons why your space program has not gotten off the ground. You will not allow yourselves to go into space without being prepared for what awaits you there. You have no idea. It is not like *Star Trek!*

Your depiction of the Enterprise is kind of like a hotel floating in space. However, space itself is not like going on a cruise. Once you leave the gravitational field of your Earth (more specifically, your solar system), you have no homing device for your consciousness. Your relationship to time, space, and self changes. You cannot go into space without being prepared for that.

We don't mean that you are going to be stopped from going into space, no. You are going to stop yourself if you are not ready. To travel in the solar system now, you may be able to rely on the gravitational fields of some of the planets for your orientation. But even then it would be difficult until your consciousness becomes more elastic.

Those of us who are in contact with humans want to prepare you for this. We want you to learn the easy way.

In order for a one-on-one contact to be meaningful, I would think there needs to be some preliminary telepathic communication first.

We would agree with you totally. All people who have any type of contact on a more physical basis have been prepared telepathically beforehand. This preparation occurs either in the dreamstate, meditation, or it is directly given to the subconscious or unconscious mind.

Much of the contact that occurs is with your future reincarnational selves. These contacts can be future Earth coming back to the 1990s (which is going on), or future Pleiadian and other races coming back to visit a past reincarnational self. If all of you had the technology right now to go back to the 1700s into a life you had in order to teach that past self, you would do it. That is what a lot of these ETs are doing. They are coming back in time to their past selves.

Let us say that you had an ET visitation from a future self. We will describe what would most likely happen: In the moment you experience that future self standing there, you would simultaneously be both people. You would be looking through your own eyes as well

15

as the eyes of the ET. The disorientation that would occur for the ego would be tremendously overpowering.

If you were an integrated being and were aware of these different aspects of yourself, the dual perception would not be as profound or disorientating. So you see, one of the reasons why the ETs are not all walking up to your back porches is because they don't want to create mass disorientation.

You mentioned Star Trek and that our experience of the Federation and of traveling through space won't be like television. Can you elaborate?

What we were saying is that if right now on Earth you had the ability to build a ship and go out into space, you would not experience a *Star Trek* reality. This is because of the present compartmentalization of your consciousness. You are not integrated, so it would be tremendously disorienting. However, as you integrate the compartments and you become more of your full self, then when you go out into space the disorientation that occurs there would be part of the natural experience and not debilitating.

If you all were *integrated* and then went out into space, then it would be similar to *Star Trek*. You would create artificial gravity and a standard time clock upon which everyone would agree. But you would have to *impose* those things into that reality because they do not occur naturally. It is not until the integration occurs that you would be able even to function enough in space to set up those constructs.

It sounds like you are describing something that is a function of emotional rather than physiological development.

Yes, although emotional development affects biochemical development. The emotional level right now is the most important. As you develop and change, your biochemical levels will change. Your brain chemistry will change. Once your brain chemistry begins to change, you will then be able to perceive multidimensionality.

You have heard about the great percentage of your brain that is not used. Often you have wondered what it is for. A significant portion of the unused areas are for multidimensional thought. Within the last year, those of you who are reading these words have used more of your brain capacity. This can be shown by your new

16

abilities to use multidimensional thought that you were not able to use a year ago.

I have often thought there are crafts masquerading as stars. Would you address this?

For the most part, our ships do not deliberately masquerade as stars. Some crafts do, however. Mostly what is happening is that the mass consciousness wants to expose itself to the energy of these ships. But right now, the mass consciousness knows no other way to do it other than to perceive them as harmless stars. Magellan's villagers were able to perceive the rowboats because they looked like their own canoes. You see crafts as stars (or airplanes) because that is the only way you can translate the energy. Again, this is not necessarily a one-on-one correlation. If Joe sees a UFO shaped like an airplane, it is not necessarily because Joe doesn't have the ability to see a spaceship. Joe reflects the whole, as a part of the mass consciousness. As the mass consciousness shifts (which it is now doing), you will start seeing other ways that this energy will manifest. The crop circles are an example. That is one idea of how the ET energy is beginning to manifest as your perceptions become more elastic.

Crop circles are very much a product of the common ground that exists between ETs and humans. Crop circles are a very deliberate attempt at communication. But this communication can be perceived now only through the use of symbology. It can't be perceived for what it truly is.

We don't want you to go overboard now, thinking that every airplane you see in the sky is a spaceship. Ultimately, it doesn't matter whether you think it is a plane or a craft. What matters is that if you feel the energy, acknowledge it within you. Let it go and don't obsess about it. That will help you develop the elasticity of your perceptions.

Is there any specific ET group who prefers to deliberately camouflage themselves?

For one thing, if we ever want to disguise ourselves, we can do it a lot more easily than to pretend we are stars! Most of the ETs with advanced technology would have the ability to simply cloak themselves. Therefore, assume that if they are camouflaging themselves, they want you to *know* they are camouflaging themselves! As to their

17

motive for wanting you to think they are camouflaged, there are as many motives as there are ETs. One might be simply to get you thinking so you can break through the wall and become more elastic.

We don't really like to speak much about the negative activities going on, because it really is such a small percentage. However, some really negative groups simply want to play with your mind. They want you to start obsessing, worrying and becoming paranoid. That generates an energy that they can use. This doesn't happen all the time, so don't be concerned about it.

Since there are so many ET groups with different motives, it gets very confusing. If we want to make contact with something, why not bypass the ETs and go directly to Source or God?

From our point of view, we don't see a difference between ETs, angels, or the Source. It is humans who create the hierarchy. It is humans who say that ETs are different from angels. You have created ETs to focus on simply to teach yourselves that nonterrestrial consciousness (angels, spirits, or God) exists. It is a tool. Once you focus on nonterrestrial consciousness, your consciousness will become more elastic. You will eventually relinquish your interest in ETs and move into other areas of interest.

We know your conscious minds may not like the following statement. Your ability to perceive nonphysicality (and the Source or God) is even farther away than your ability to perceive ETs. Learning to perceive ETs is a stepping stone to even greater perceptions about creation and God. One step at a time!

Are there other planets who are in a similar stage of evolution as Earth?

Every culture is unique, and certainly that includes Earth. You are a product of several things. First, you are a product of the natural indigenous species that evolved on Earth. You are also a product of genetic engineering by many ET races. Your unique combination of genetics is not similar to that of any other planet. Most planets are more homogeneous in their genetics. You have been the product of so many genetic projects that it is one big melting pot here.

I personally have been involved in several first-contact missions. This requires that I assist in preparing a planet for its entrance into the galactic community. Generally, it is a fairly short period of time

18

that is required for such a preparation. Your planet has been the most difficult.

For example, most planets have a single planetary language. A language reflects the perceptions of its user. So when I go to a planet for a first-contact mission, I know the perceptions of the people on the planet by studying the language. When we come to Earth, there are hundreds of languages and dialects that we encounter. They all reflect different perceptions. We know that many of you have noticed themes in contact cases. For instance, South America has a certain theme. If you were to study all the contact cases all over the world (by Pleiadians), you will conclude that the language spoken by the contactees will be a deciding factor in creating the theme of the contact.

When we come to Earth, it is very difficult and we have to proceed very carefully. We cannot afford to misunderstand you. We cannot afford to misperceive your reality.

How do you interpret us? How do you deal with all of our languages?

Well, we do have linguistic specialists. Generally a linguistic specialist can learn an Earth language fluently within one cycle of your moon. Once the linguist can learn the language, we can then begin to crack what we call "perceptual codings." These perceptual codings are much more important for us to learn than the actual language itself. Then we formulate our methods of contact. That is not my department, however, because I am not a linguist.

Remember that earlier we were talking about shamans. Shamans are the people in your culture who serve as a lens. They assimilate our energy and filter it through themselves into your mass consciousness. (This is like filtering it through the Earth perceptions.) This is why shamans (or people like them) are the ones to be contacted first. We can equate this channel (and many others) to the shamans as well. Channels and your contemporary shamans are the lenses through which new perceptions of reality are disseminated to your mass consciousness. It comes through channeling, Native American teachings, visionary art, and much more.

In closing we will say that just by the material you've read in this chapter, your perceptions have become more elastic. This will continue as you seek to expand the boundaries of your own consciousness. This can be an exciting journey! Along this journey, we bid you well. ∇

2
Exploring the Contact Experience

"... we could be in the beginning stages of a major shift in levels of consciousness that will eventually lead to humanity's being able to live in two worlds at once ..."

— Kenneth Ring, Ph.D.
The Omega Project

If we could understand the mechanics of contact with extraterrestrials, perhaps we could understand more about human consciousness. Why are so many contacts revealed only through regressive hypnosis?

It seems that there is a whole dimension of the human experience that occurs outside the reaches of our conscious minds. Indications seem clear that human consciousness is compartmentalized in such a way as to protect the ego from threatening or confusing stimuli. If this is true, we might be having ongoing and meaningful contact with extraterrestrials (among other types of beings) constantly, as part of our natural subconscious or unconscious life. Do we in fact have a secret life? Or several?

In this chapter, Sasha begins to address alternate views of reality that do not fit the Western model. These alternate views of reality may provide us with useful insight into the deeper workings of the human mind and the unlimited possibilities for extraterrestrial contact.

Δ   Δ   Δ

You mentioned how significant a change in consciousness is in order to bring about contact. Would people who alter their consciousness be the actual contactees?

Sasha: Not necessarily. It all depends on who needs what experience for their own growth. So it could very likely be, for example, that the people who needed the contact or the people who co-created the contact or agreed to the contact are people who may not ever embrace the steps given in Chapter One. It is not necessarily going to be the ones who embrace the steps who draw the contact to themselves, but they will be the ones instrumental in drawing the contact to humanity itself.

What are some ways of contacting extraterrestrials besides channeling?

The first thing we have to explain here is that no one can *make* contact happen. It's not going to be a magic pill that you take or a magic dance that you do out in the desert that will draw them to you. If you have an agreement (conscious or unconscious) to experience extraterrestrial contact, you are going to do it whether you are sitting in a closet or out in the desert every night. So the idea of making it happen by doing certain techniques, as if you must push certain buttons, is not going to be that reliable, because each person will go through the process of pushing those buttons for their own purposes. The goal mustn't be the end result, but the growth process and the learning you experience. Otherwise there will always be disappointment.

In terms of other ways to facilitate contact, we are going to reword the question. You would like to know how to best prepare yourself for contact, and how to create a fertile ground upon which contact can occur. We have much to say on this matter, and it will be addressed in the coming chapters. First, we are assuming that the kind of contact you desire is face to face.

A note of caution here. We remind you that we give you this information because this *process* is valuable for your own evolution. We do not give you this information for you to *make* contact happen. You needn't worry about being heard by us. **We hear you.** However, do you always answer your phone every time it rings? If you do not, it is not necessarily because you don't like the person on the other end. Sometimes it is simply not a good time to pick up the phone. Remember this analogy when you shake your fists at the sky waiting for us to answer you!

One of the most profound ways to get you closer to open contact is to investigate your own previous contacts that may have escaped attention from your conscious mind. We suggest that you investigate through regressive hypnosis or through guided meditation any types of extraterrestrial contact of which you have previously been un-aware. (A competent hypnotherapist can greatly assist you with this.) This is going to start unlocking doorways within you so that you will become more receptive to extraterrestrial frequencies. Then you may begin to be able to tune in to the presence of extraterrestrial craft a lot easier, once you are acclimated to the vibration through your own hypnotic explorations. Because you will begin to recognize the vibrations, the repressed memories will surface even more. You will become much more aware of how the extraterrestrial thread has run through your life already, and in that case your reality will be more perceptive to ET contact. Please remember that ET contact will not necessarily conform to your rules of physicality!

Now, here's another idea that is very challenging to understand. When people say they want contact, they imagine contact in a context they can imagine. For instance, the common theme of contact one might imagine goes something like this: The person is sitting out in the desert. A ship lands. An entity comes out and talks to them or communicates in some way, and the ship leaves. That imaginary contact is a product of your own mass consciousness and your own limitations on your perceptions of reality. It is assumed by many that these types of contacts will be recalled by the conscious mind, so that you will retain the memory of that contact just like you remember going to the grocery store yesterday.

This premise has gotten you in a lot of trouble. Any other type of extraterrestrial interaction that may have happened is then discarded as noncontact. Yet contact itself does not conform to the rules of your reality, and it certainly does not conform to the boundaries you have placed on your consciousness! So more likely than not, right now in the mass consciousness, if any given person experienced the landing of a ship in the desert complete with an ET meeting, the mind itself will need to compartmentalize the memory in order to digest it, integrate it and incorporate it into the being. This means it is very likely that the memory itself will not be consciously recalled.

So we're back to the frustrating concept that you cannot really force contact. *Contact could have already happened to you, unbeknownst to your conscious mind.* You may not ever know it has happened, and you may continually be trying to force it to no avail. The evolution of your own consciousness has not yet gotten to the point where contact can be totally accepted. Therefore, the most logical next step is to *prepare* your consciousness to accept contact on all levels. It is only then that you will become aware of the contact that has already happened and be ready for the contact that awaits you. Ninety percent of the people on your planet have already had contact in one way, shape or form already!

Let us address for a moment the tools that many think can bring about contact. One is no more valuable than another. We will use Joe as an example. Let us say he is absolutely convinced that if he goes out in the desert and does a rain dance and stands on his head for two hours he is going to bring about contact. That will be his tool, and it is as valuable as anything else. So it's not a matter of finding a process outside of you that works. *It's a matter of finding a process internally that works.* We as extraterrestrials don't care what kind of rain dances you do. We don't care what kind of radio waves you beam to us. What we do respond to is your inner frequency, your inner desire, your inner evolution and your inner integrity. Without that you can be sending messages in a bottle throughout infinity, but we are not going to answer.

How important or necessary is the drinking of pure water in relationship to making conscious physical contact with ETs?

Drinking pure water is not necessary, but it does speed up the process of your own detoxification, which of course would be detoxification emotionally as well as physically. The detoxification emotionally will clear you and allow you to be able to interact with us more easily. Although it's not essential that you drink pure water, it will be beneficial to you in the long run in terms of your level of detoxification. That will allow you to be a more clear receiver of communication, whether it's physical or nonphysical.

If a group uses certain meditations or techniques, would its chance of a close encounter be greater than for a group of skywatchers? If so, would you say that by increasing the intensity of those methods would it in turn increase the chance of a close encounter?

24

The answer to that question, as we perceive it, is no. This goes back to what we have just said. If it is going to happen, it is going to happen no matter what rain dance you are doing. Let's take a group of people and put them into hypothetical situations. Let's say that on this arbitrary Tuesday night they are sitting in their house and with this big device, and they're trying to call the ETs. Let's say that in a parallel reality they are out skywatching, not doing anything specific, just lying in lawnchairs looking at the sky. So the question becomes, "Which reality will call the ETs?" The answer is neither, either, or both—it really doesn't matter. If contact is going to happen, it is going to happen no matter what they are doing. It is more *likely* to happen in whichever reality they are expressing more of their true selves and their excitement.

Contact occurs at a time of readiness, and whatever you're doing at that time does not matter. However, if your group is excited to follow a certain procedure or meditation, then the learning of that procedure is what is needed to actually help you energetically move through the seven steps Germane has talked about. The specific technology you use is not important. *What is essential, however, is the internal process you experience as you prepare for contact.*

There is nothing you can do outside of yourself and your own evolutionary process that will bring about the contact. There has been an assumption on your planet that extraterrestrials don't hear you and that if they could just *hear* you they would communicate. Well, we hear you very loudly, but what we hear is not what you think you are putting out. That is where some of the confusion lies. Your devices do not serve to call us, but they may help you get through an evolutionary process.

What methods, such as lights, the playing of crop circle sounds and meditation, is the most vital for contacting the ETs?

We have just stated that there is no magic button. The important factor is *you* rather than your procedures. Let us reword the question: *Which method will assist you in acclimating yourself to an ET vibration?* First of all we would say the most vital or the most efficient is the evolving of the self. We must always suggest that you allow the first step to be an internal process. If you focus on the external, contact is not going to happen.

Each person or group will have their own keys to unlock contact, and this key will be a product of their own growth and resonance field. When this key is used, it will simply unlock your own consciousness to be able to receive information and communication from other levels of consciousness (ETs included). There is no single skeleton key that opens the universe. Whenever anyone believes that there's only one key to anything, then that one key can be controlled and withheld from you.

Can the combination of lights and sounds nudge the brain into a state receptive for contact?

Yes. This will be explored even further in later chapters. The alpha brain-wave state occurs during meditation or day dreaming. The theta brain-wave state occurs in deep meditation. It is also known as the threshold between waking and sleeping. In our understanding, the theta state in humans is when most contacts occur. If you compare the theta state with the process of falling asleep, this is the period that some people call hypnogogic. In this state humans often have bizarre waking dreams, and if they're able to wake up before they fall into normal sleep, they may remember some of these or it may be very distorted. This is the same brain-wave state where a good portion of the contacts occur.

You will begin to remember your contacts more clearly if you can do the following: (1) Train yourself to achieve theta consciousness and maintain it without falling asleep; (2) train yourself while in theta to slide into the simultaneous reality in which many of the ETs exist; (3) communicate there with us and then bring the memory back to your conscious mind. If this can be achieved, you will very rapidly begin an open contact program beyond what you have imagined thus far. This is not necessarily an easy task, nor is it a necessary one, but it is just one of those many keys.

If a close encounter of the fifth kind is to occur before a group of people, would precontact communication be needed between the ETs and the group so that there can be a mutual understanding of the groundwork details, such as landing sites, security arrangements, etc.?

It is our understanding that before any type of major contact would occur with a group of people, the precontact will already have happened. This precontact will be most likely on the telepathic level.

26

This telepathic communication may not necessarily be recalled on the conscious level. Again, we're back to the compartmentalization of the human consciousness, which for us is very difficult to work around. If the human does not remember the precontact communication, he or she may feel unconsciously compelled to do certain things. For instance, maybe one night Joe invites a group of friends into the desert. Let's say that Joe inadvertently leaves out one friend by forgetting to call him. Let's say they go out to the desert and the contact occurs. Now, it's very likely that the precontact communication said that this person who was forgotten should not be present. This is just an example. So even though the precontact message was not remembered, it was inadvertently carried out.

You as humans will always carry out what the greater portion of yourself knows needs to happen. When your conscious mind struggles for control of the entire situation, you're literally taking yourself further away from the contact.

Regarding your statements about security arrangements, we are aware of movies on your planet that depict things like this. An example is your film *Close Encounters of the Third Kind*. That movie, with all respect to you, was humorous in a very warm way to us, because most of us would not ever agree to a contact that was orchestrated like that unless we knew it was part of some type of propaganda that would eventually be good for you.

It still seems quite logical to at least have some contact scenarios the way we would want them.

Yes, all right. Some contact scenarios *will* happen for you according to the way you think they should. This is not because we require this, but because *you* require it.

We prefer that the human participants are neutral and not associated with any type of military or governmental structure. If we were to arrange our most perfect contact, we would like a linguist there. We would like an anthropologist there. We would like a physicist there. We would like a telepath there. We would like children there. We would like dolphins there. We would like people there who are not going to revere us as gods. Though this spontaneous mix of beings is unlikely from your point of view, this is not something that is impossible.

27

We are not as anxious for contact as many of you are. We have a little bit more of a bird's-eye view, so we're not as impatient.

The more that humans can connect with our reality, the more likely you will bring contact about. Planning things too rigidly will actually push the contact further from you. We know that sounds almost like a paradox but . . .

It's an attempt to bind and control the future.

And since we live only in the present and do not worry about our future, this is not compatible.

How would you respond if I said that on behalf of all humans interested in initiating extraterrestrial contact, you are hereby cordially invited to visit our planet openly?

First of all, we are very honored and grateful for the invitation. We have already accepted the invitation, but in your terms right now we are taking a raincheck. This is not saying that you are not good enough or that we are waiting for you to grow up or anything like that. Let us illustrate what we mean by an analogy.

The analogy is that we on our end are preparing for contact. We do not necessarily just get in our ships and land. The process looks like this: Right now we are washing our cars and we are filling our tanks with gas. We are preparing for the road trip to visit you. But we know we can't arrive until a certain time. It would be no use in getting into the car and driving to your house because when we got to the destination no one would be home anyway, and we would end up having to stay in a hotel. What we are implying is that when we do visit and say, "Here we are," you don't see us, you don't sense us, and to some degree we can barely see you, because the frequencies have not aligned yet.

This has nothing to do with judgment. It's simply that the frequencies do not yet match. People have asked us, "Sasha, why are you holding back?" We're not holding back! The realities don't connect yet, and the way for the realities to begin to connect will be when you begin embracing certain concepts such as the information in Chapter One. We will begin connecting when you begin to identify yourselves as a planetary species. That's the key for when our realities are going to start lining up together. And once that happens, contact will be

28

inevitable. We are not going to suddenly decide to land one day. *We are already here, and you will begin to see us.*

So the imagined ways of contact that you perpetuate through your fiction and conversation are not the way it is going to come about. But the imagined ways of contact are necessary to prepare you internally for what is to come.

Sasha, let's play a little game, but it can be as real as it needs to be. Let's get into the mind of a Pleiadian. Imagine that there is a ship in the area. What would compel a pilot to make a visible contact with a human?

All right, imagine this: You are a ship in the middle of the ocean, and you are in a very deep, thick fog. You are radioing and flashing your lights, but no one can see you. You can't see anyone else, either. But suddenly there's a break in the fog and you see a light. You immediately move toward that light, and you attempt to make contact. When we come to your planet, we're in a fog. Your mass consciousness is somewhat like a fog to us. When a light breaks free of the fog and we perceive it, then we know because of our perception that the contact is an appropriate action to take. Most of the time, however, the fog is so great that we cannot distinguish the shore from a boat in your mass consciousness.

Let's take an example where this has already happened. I'm sure you know some Pleiadians who have had a visual exchange with a human. Let's talk about this situation. How did it align, and what was the Pleiadian thinking and feeling?

The Pleiadian, first of all, was totally in the flow. I am thinking specifically of an incident that occurred in a remote area of the outback in Australia with a colleague of mine. One of the things that my colleague does is make contact and maintain relationships with what you would call holy people, medicine men, or shamans on your planet. In this particular case, the ship simply landed in the desert and the shaman knew the ship was coming. The shaman just knew psychically, and my friend of course knew that the shaman expected her.

There is a sense of total synchronicity unlike anything most of you on your planet know now. Because of the advanced abilities of the shaman, he was much more able to perceive a fourth-density type of reality. The interaction occurred in what this Aborigine shaman would call the dreamtime. The medicine man was not sleeping, but he entered an altered reality state that could be likened to the theta state. The theta state of consciousness exists outside of the normal flow of your waking consciousness, which is the beta brain wave state.

This contact was physical, and my friend had a physical conversation with the shaman. But when my colleague left, the shaman exited the dreamtime and entered a different dream — the dream of humanity — and he was able to relay his interaction with the Pleiadian through his own words in his own culture as a dreamtime experience. The dreamtime for the Aborigine is *not* the Western version of a dream, which you do not think is real. The dreamtime is as real as the waking time.

Although that is certainly valid, it does me little good. For one thing, I'm not a shaman, I'm not Aborigine, I'm not in Australia, and I can barely remember my dreams!

Dreamtime is not dreams. It's not when you are asleep and dreaming. That's not what we mean by dreamtime. Any human is perfectly able to train themselves to reach theta and alter their consciousness in order to have a dreamtime experience. It is simply a matter of retraining yourself and de-anchoring yourself to the physical illusion. All humans in your society who are contacted by us physically have the ability of de-anchoring themselves. That's the reason why they are contacted and can maintain memory (which is a rare quality). They do, in a sense, enter their own type of dreamtime, a Western version of dreamtime where the brain frequency is changed.

So doesn't the actual physical presence of an extraterrestrial compel the human to enter into dreamtime?

Yes, yes!

So is that why there is trauma after some contact experiences?

Yes. When shamans are apprentices, one of the things that they have to confront is their own darkness and fears. This is because when they enter the dreamtime, their own demons go with them. These demons are much more real in the dreamtime than they are in the waking time. So when one of these extraterrestrials interacts with you, it thrusts you into the dreamtime, and in that dreamtime your whole concept of reality is altered.

30

If your normal waking life is very solidly grounded in waking time, this is going to be a shock. It is very likely that your memory will compartmentalize and you will not be able to access further memory of the experience. However, if you're unplugged from the waking time and you really exist in a type of quasi-dreamtime reality and if you're de-anchored, you'll be much more likely to retain memory of the experience, or at least memory that the experience happened.

Could you give me an example of a contact that happened with a typical person with a Western consciousness?

The first story that comes to mind is simply of a woman in a metropolitan area of your United States of America. One evening she was at her office working late, and she was the only one in the office. A Pleiadian female came into the office, and as she did, the woman became very sleepy. This is a very common human response to our presence, because it is a way for the human to integrate and process the experience. The woman interacted with the Pleiadian from that groggy state. The human remained in that state for the duration of the contact.

Now, this was a contact simply of future self (Pleiadian) to past self (human), and did not have any significant societal importance in that sense.

What was the Pleiadian wearing?

At first when she came into the office she was dressed in a man's business suit, and this type of subtle strangeness was enough to shift the human into the dreamtime. Then the Pleiadian woman started to change more into her natural appearance, wearing a simple tunic and leggings.

Why did this Pleiadian want the woman to enter into the dreamtime?

The Pleiadian didn't necessarily want it. It is the natural thing that happens when two beings of different realities meet. They find a common ground. After the interaction occurred, the Pleiadian woman left and the woman awoke several hours later on the couch in her office and just assumed that she had fallen asleep. She never really gave it much thought.

Perhaps now you can see what we mean by the compartmentaliza-tion of consciousness. These types of contacts happen more fre-

31

quently than you realize. The human brain has an automatic ability to screen out all perceptions that do not adhere to its standards of normalcy. This is certainly something that has been proven over and over again in your psychological research. As you begin to pay more attention to the subtleties of your consciousness and seek to expand it into more and more distant realms, there are many surprises that await you. ∇

3
The Dream

"As long as the formlessness and breathtaking freedom of the beyond remain frightening to us, we will continue to dream a hologram for ourselves that is comfortably solid and well defined."

— Michael Talbot
The Holographic Universe

The brain is the central processing unit for our entire experience as humans. The brain regulates our growth, stores our memory, and translates a chaotic array of sensory images into a coherent perception of reality. As amazing as the brain is, could it be possible that our brain may also limit our perceptions of reality as well?

Within the contact experience, it is obvious that we do not have all the answers. Contactees are bombarded with images and experiences that the most advanced of our sciences cannot even begin to understand. But one thing is clear; these contact experiences *are* happening. We need a tool that will help us begin to make sense of this confusing panoply of stimuli. Could it be that the tool we seek is locked within each person — the human brain?

Researchers have long known that brain conditions affect reality perception. If this is truly the case, then it would stand to reason that if our brains were trained to interact differently with consciousness and reality, we might finally be able to discover some concrete truths about ET contact. As long as we continue to view reality through our current use of brain power, these answers may elude us forever.

Our conversations with Sasha have allowed us to conclude that the ET contact phenomenon is actually serving to stimulate a metamorphosis of consciousness within humans. It has become clear that as our brains develop, so does our ability to perceive new levels of reality. Until now it is as if we have been underwater. We have been trying to see above the surface of the water from under the water itself. A tremendous amount of distortion has colored our perceptions of what exists above the surface. However, if we can learn to adjust our perceptual abilities enough to stick our heads out of the water, a whole new reality will be viewed. Our ET contacts are catalyzing us toward these discoveries. The *more* confused we become about ET contact, the *more* ET contact will appear in our reality. It is *forcing us* to elasticize our perceptions.

If this is in fact true, then we are in a transitional period. In such a period it would be natural to expect confusion until we adjust to our new perceptual abilities. As you will read in this chapter, Sasha discusses the process of awakening from our old "dream" of reality into a new level of awareness. These ideas will be addressed even further in following chapters.

Δ Δ Δ

Sasha: We would like to continue with the story about Magellan.

If you remember, in Chapter One we told you about Magellan's experience on a remote island and how the natives could not see his great sailing ship on the horizon. These natives could, however, see the rowboats that he and his men came to shore in because those rowboats were similar to their own canoes. They were not able to see the large ship because their reality construct was such that they could not perceive something so alien to them.

That interpretation is true. However, we're going to give you another point of view that does not discount the previous point of view but simply adds to it. We've talked somewhat about the evolution of the human species. One of the things that humans are finding the most challenging right now (which of course is a product of your evolutionary stage), is the compartmentalization of your consciousness. This means that your waking consciousness, your unconscious, and your dream world are all separated by certain boundaries. Those boundaries, at least for now in the reality framework you're living in, have helped you make sense of the world in which you live. These boundaries have helped you to process energy and new ideas at a rate that is safe for you. This rate of processing correlates to your brain development.

Each of these states of consciousness (whether it is the dream state or the waking state) is a product of brain-wave frequency. You could also call it vibrational frequency, for it is basically the same thing. Humans, for their own purposes, have limited themselves to certain brain-wave frequencies for their primary expressions. This will be dealt with more in later chapters, but for now we will categorize them once again.

The **beta** state is the brain-wave that is dominant when you are awake. The **alpha** state is the brain-wave state that you fall into when you are daydreaming, meditating, fantasizing, and sometimes even watching TV. The **delta** state is the sleep state. The **theta** state is the doorway or the bridge between alpha and delta. When brain waves shift (for instance, from beta to alpha), the brain literally begins emitting a whole new frequency. This frequency determines the type of reality that the human will experience. Because of the differences in these frequencies and the way the brain shifts between them, boundaries can be maintained around the compartments of your consciousness.

From our point of view, humans generate the most brain-wave activity in the theta state of consciousness — therefore, theta is most dominant. From the human point of view, you are only awake and functioning and connected with your ego in the beta state, so to you beta is the dominant state. However, the beta reality represents a very small fraction of your brain's total capacity to generate and perceive other realities.

Therefore, because the illusion exists for humans that the beta/waking state is the most dominant, you will assume that all of your significant or valid interactions with other beings (physical or nonphysical) must occur during the beta/waking state. From our point of view this is really an absurd belief, because the beta-generated reality represents only a very small percentage of your entire capacity.

Humans have put much time and energy into the study of the UFO phenomenon, and they have attempted to come up with some type of logical understanding about how and why contact occurs. But in your theories you have validated only the beta/waking reality, and thus have come up far short of any serious understanding of ET contact. This is because most of your contact does not occur in that very limited beta brain-wave frequency.

We as Pleiadians do not operate in such a refined and limited frequency as beta. We do not have the rigid divisions between levels of consciousness that you have. If we were to communicate with humans on the beta frequency, it would require a tremendous alteration to our energy, consciousness, and reality construct. We cannot hold the energy necessary to communicate on that rigid beta frequency. For this reason, the greater portion of extraterrestrial communication has occurred on other levels of consciousness — the alpha, the theta and also the delta. Overall, the majority of our contacts occur within the theta frequency because it is a common ground that we both can reach.

This brings us back to one of the most common questions asked of us by humans: "Well, Sasha, if I don't remember it, how do I know I have had a contact?" or "If I don't remember contact, how can I accept it as valid?" You have every right to choose not to validate unremembered contact; however, that choice and the adherence to that choice will severely handicap your ability to maintain relations with any type of extraterrestrial consciousness.

Let us describe for a moment some more qualities of the theta state. Theta is what many people have called the hypnogogic state, the state between sleeping and waking, the state that for most people cannot be controlled. It is a state that you pass through on your way to sleep, but you do not necessarily utilize it for anything but the vehicle to get you from waking to sleeping. In the last 20 years there has been a lot more research on the theta state, and many more people have been willing (whether through meditation or through the use of technological devices) to experiment with their theta states. These people have found tremendous benefits and significant changes in their levels of consciousness. This is because they've begun dissolving the wall, so to speak, between all the levels of consciousness. By consciously engaging in the theta level from a conscious, beta-oriented decision, they've begun to integrate the levels of consciousness and the boundaries begin to disintegrate. (We will speak even more about contact and the brain in later chapters.)

The people on your planet who are more likely to be receptive to benevolent, face to face extraterrestrial contact are those individuals who are adept at functioning on the theta level. These people will be able to filter the essence of that contact into their waking selves (their beta level), because the walls between levels will begin to dissolve. This will result in actual remembered contacts and the realization that these contacts have been going on all along.

When a planet is getting ready for extraterrestrial contact and contact with new levels of reality, the brains of the species on the planet begin evolving rapidly. This is happening right now on Earth. As the brains begin evolving to another level, a new subspecies begins to emerge through a kind of subtle mutation. When this begins to happen, the brain-wave capacity of the human changes, and therefore their ability to perceive other levels of reality begins changing. It is then that they realize the **extraterrestrials are not going to suddenly appear to humans; rather, humans will begin to perceive the ET contact which has gone on all along.**

We are observing that on your planet now a significant number of people are experiencing this rapid brain evolution. This results in an increased ability for humans to consciously control their brain-wave states. This is being shown in your biofeedback research. These new abilities are beginning to open new doorways in multidimensional perception—which in turn is really putting a new light on the extraterrestrial phenomenon.

Contact is possible on the beta level, but as we've said previously, it's very difficult from the point of view of the extraterrestrials because it means entering an extremely refined frequency. You will find that the lesser-evolved extraterrestrial species (those who are more closely matched to your own evolutionary time line) will have less difficulty entering the beta reality. These ETs will be able to maintain themselves longer in your beta frequency.

However, the more evolved extraterrestrial entities (those who have had more time for evolution), will find it difficult to interact on your beta level. Therefore if it becomes essential to do so, they may instead temporarily disguise themselves in a subtly strange way. For the human, the subtle strangeness of the event will cause a relaxing of the beta frequencies. The human's brain-waves will begin changing subtly so that the communication can occur without those rigid constraints that exist in beta.

For instance, an extraterrestrial may enter the reality of the human in the guise of a human astronaut, a mystic, or an eccentric. The unconscious of the human will perceive the ET energy. The conscious mind will only perceive the *strangeness* of the event, but it will be enough to trigger the person into a more receptive state (such as alpha). That in turn will allow the communication to be much more effective.

Can you accomplish this artificially by using a device or a synthetic person to enter that beta realm?

Synthetic people are used sometimes for contacts and that is a logical reason why. Again, it depends on the specific extraterrestrial society that is involved. Synthetic people have been used, though even in our technological age they are not perfected and are not agile enough for our purposes.

What about holograms?

Holograms are wonderful to convey information, but at this point the hologram does not carry the energy essence of the sender. Because of this, to the human perceiver it's less real. Humans sometimes do not even perceive projected holograms because of the absence of lifeforce. So holograms are not reliable, either. The main difficulty we have in making open contact with you is the differences in the frequencies of our reality and yours as well as the differences in frequency between our brain-wave states and yours. Many people have thought that we're not here because we judge you as unworthy, or because you're not ready, or a myriad of other reasons. Some of those may be accurate reasons for certain extraterrestrial species, but not us. The best answer as to why contact is not open and ongoing right now is that our realities can't connect yet. The brain-wave functioning between us is so different at this point that if we could simply *perceive* each other clearly, it would be a tremendous accomplishment.

This is why so many of the extraterrestrials seem so interested in your spiritual development. It's not that we're on some galactic evangelical crusade for new-age thinking! It is simply that the less rigid you become in your belief systems, the more fluid you are in the different levels of your consciousness. Once that happens, you will open up more and then be able to perceive us. That is a tremendous motivation for us. We don't want to spread the "truth" of the universe, so to speak, but simply help you open a crack in the door so that you can perceive a greater reality and then make your own decisions.

Why not use a lesser-evolved species to contact us for you?

Your question implies that we're desperate to have communication and that we do not perceive that there is a flow. There is an evolutionary flow here that we respect. For us to use a lesser-evolved species and force something that's not there naturally, in an evolutionary sense, is to say that we don't respect your own timing.

Our world is not as easily accessible from the outside as we might think it is. It is like we are dreaming and in a way you're trying to wake us up from a bad dream. But in order to wake us up, you are not willing to enter the dream with us.

Exactly. Very good analogy. We have not spoken of this before, but some of us have entered your bad dreams, so to speak. In our past, these ETs were not able to find their way out. They became confused. This is not a very common occurrence. There are stories about it in our history.

We do not want to enter your dream. However, we can play the role of your mother shaking you and saying, "It's time to get up, it's time to get up!" Ultimately you are the one who says, "Five more minutes, please." So you've set your species clock on snooze, and that's all right. That's what you need for now.

So do all species have their own dream? This means that contact between one group of evolved extraterrestrials and another is not as easy as we might think it is?

That is accurate. Any time you enter physical reality, you're entering a dream, an illusion. So the most densely physical societies are going to have the most densely physical dreams. And they're not necessarily even going to be aware that it is a dream. So entering someone else's dream requires a tremendous amount of focus. It also requires a tremendous amount of self-identity to be able to pull yourself out of the dream if you get in too far.

There are many stories in your culture about extraterrestrial contact with the benevolent space brothers flying to your planet, landing

39

and shaking hands. There are many other levels that must be dealt with. These other aspects have to do with the differences in reality framework. It's not as simple as it may seem.

So each civilization has its own dream. If the dreams are similar enough then would contact be easy and supportive?

That is it. If the dreams are similar enough to each other, then the contact is very easy. But if the dreams vary in intensity, it's much more challenging. Instead of trying to muster the energy and the will to enter your dream, it's much easier for us to help you learn that you're sleeping and dreaming and then give you the choice to wake up if you like. That helps you maintain your own free will. It is not our duty to impose on you that you must awaken; instead, we want to give you an opportunity to awaken if you desire.

Ultimately, we cannot ever communicate to you that you are in a dream. You have all had sleeping dreams where in the dream you've said, "Oh, I'm dreaming. This is all part of the dream," but instead of waking up you have simply gone on with the dream. We cannot communicate to you from outside of the dream. We can only communicate to you from *inside* the dream. This is one of the reasons why channels are so helpful in relaying messages from us. Even though during channeling we are seemingly communicating to you from inside the dream, we can also be likened to a periscope. We are underwater with you, but we also still retain our cosmic sight. We don't have to enter the dream through channeling in order to communicate with you.

Is this why there's a necessary distortion in channeling — because there's a distortion in this reality?

There is a distortion in this reality. Simply put, if you try to shoot a fish with a bow and arrow, the water creates a distortion. Unless you know how to compensate, you're most likely going to miss the fish.

We are looking at you through a distortion. Unless we know exactly how to compensate, what you receive will always be distorted according to your own perceptions of reality. Right now the distortion is becoming less and less, but it's still there and we do the best we can.

So you do think there is progress being made?

Absolutely so, yes. The level of distortion is decreasing rapidly. In studying the human brain-wave capabilities, we're seeing marked changes in your abilities to consciously hold and maintain both alpha and theta state. Beta is not as dominant as it used to be. So the levels are starting to blend, which means the walls are starting to come down. This in and of itself creates a domino effect. This is one of the key dominos that will shift everything on your planet.

Is this why other Earth cultures who might not be so focused in beta seem to have more ET contact?

Yes. You will notice that indigenous species (such as your Aborigine and Native American) have many, many contacts. These contacts are not talked about or written about as being strange, because it is something that has happened to them for generations. Earth's indigenous races have fewer barriers between the different levels of consciousness. Alpha and theta are not as alien to them as they are to Western society, so you're going to find more contact going on there. However, you may not ever hear about it.

Contact between indigenous tribes and Western culture has had a severe and often overwhelming impact on them. So what kind of effect has ET contact had with the same people?

Do you know why Western civilization has had an overwhelming effect on the indigenous people? Because Western society and the indigenous people are living a different dream. Extraterrestrials visiting the indigenous peoples are less alien to them than your own Western society is.

Technology has often been thought to be the symbol of intelligence, but it is not. True harmonious technology is the result of understanding universal laws and *feeling* that truth within your being. The true extension of that knowledge can stimulate the creation of harmonious technology. Western civilization has forced technology — not from an understanding of universal law but to test universal law and prove universal theory. The indigenous people (which includes cetaceans) have a sensing, a knowingness, a trust of the universal laws. And from that point of balance they have the choice to extend that into technology or not. *Both choices are equal.* The indigenous peoples have chosen instead to balance the technological imbalance on Earth by maintaining nontechnological societies.

Please do not misunderstand that we think you should become like the indigenous peoples. You will naturally flow in the direction you need to. However, at this point one of the most significant things that can be done to aid the evolution of your entire species is any type of brain-evolving activity that will allow you to begin perceiving multi-dimensional reality.

Let's say I am an ET and I want to communicate into someone else's dream. What could I do? Ah ha! I could leave drawings in their dream! That's just what crop circles are, aren't they?

That is one reason for them, yes! The crop circles have symbolism on many levels for you, and that is one level, yes. We are not able to tell you exactly what the crop circles are saying because you are in your dream and we are in ours. It would not make sense yet. All we can say is that you're pointed in the right direction, but any words that you give to it right now cannot be the exact message because you're still in the dream. For now we will say that the crop circles are a calling card or a signpost that can lead you out of the dream. V

4

Mechanics of First Contact:
A Case Study

"Only by confronting and yielding to the unknowable — by rigorously avoiding both the temptation to deny or explain away these phenomena or to try to find some conventional explanation for them — can we, as a species, evolve . . ."

— Kenneth Ring, Ph.D.
The Omega Project

Humans spend so much time and energy wondering about the reality of extraterrestrial contact. When will open contact happen? What is the protocol of a contact between humans and extraterrestrials? Where will it happen?

Up until now we have not put as much effort into imagining the logistics of contact — from an extraterrestrial's point of view. What do they have to do in order to open contact? What are their philosophies and how are these philosophies played out in the contact scenario?

In this chapter Sasha gives the reader an inside look at contact protocol. She recounts a recent contact mission that was relatively effortless to illuminate the step-by-step process that occurs during a first-contact mission. She gives this information also with the desire to communicate the importance of flexibility of consciousness during any contact with extraterrestrials.

Δ   Δ   Δ

Sasha: I often participate in first-contact missions. There is a recent mission I would like to discuss with you. This star is located about 50,000 light years from Earth. With your strongest telescopes

43

you would be able to see the star, but it would seem very, very insignificant. Its magnitude is very similar to your Sol, although the star is slightly smaller in diameter. The star is a little bit greener, but very close to the color of yours.

There are branches of the Association of Worlds that operate primarily in that sector of this galaxy. A branch of the Association has been watching this planet for quite some time. It was being monitored because its evolution suddenly picked up speed at an extraordinary rate. The Association has been looking for the most advantageous time in which to make open contact. When it was seen that it was time, they put out the word, so to speak, through the Association for volunteers for the contact team. This project excited me greatly because it would eventually include open, face to face contact, which was something I had not done up to this point. My methods of contact have usually been through the use of telepathy and dream work, so this was an opportunity for me to venture into an area that was very new, but at the same time very exciting.

Were you aware of this society before the contact mission?

I had been aware of reports that circulate through the Association on a regular basis that have to do with different worlds and what progress they are making. I was aware of them only through research. But I had never had any hands-on experience with them.

These beings are humanoid — two arms, two legs, a head. They also could be considered somewhat Aryan in nature, being that they are primarily light-skinned with light hair. They are also very slender and ectomorphic.

Once the volunteer team got together, we had to assign roles for each of us. Because of my extensive work with telepaths, it was obvious that I would still work with the telepaths from their society.

The first-contact team was made up of several species. I was one of the very few of direct Pleiadian/Lyran lineage. So it was also very obvious that I would then be part of the first-contact, face to face team because of my physiological similarity to them. Had there been another choice, the most obvious would have been someone who was taller than I. But I resembled their species enough, so it wasn't threatening.

We are going to call these people the **Zenah**. (Do not be overly

44

attached to the label. It is a vibrational resonance that has meaning for them.) The first-contact team was sent to study the Zenah. We studied them for two cycles of their moon. This was an intensive study. Our linguists learned the language of the planet, because when one understands the language of a planet one also understands its people. What we found, in comparison to Earth, is that they were slightly more evolved. Please do not take that in a judgmental way. They are older, and there are several main differences between you and them.

One difference is that they have one planetary language. This was something that caused a lot of disagreement in their past. However, it was decided that it would be beneficial and unifying for the planet to have one language. The planetary language was implemented about 100 of their years ago. The people of the planet have since learned to communicate with each other globally. This, of course, changes the brain chemistry, which in turn creates more of a sense of unification.

They also had only one religion on the planet. Individuals either believed in that religion or had their personal sense of spirituality. On Zenah the people never fought about religion. From the early days they had always felt that religion was a very personal thing. You can see how that could save a lot of strife in a society.

In their sector of the galaxy they are somewhat isolated and there had not been a lot of extraterrestrial visitations. There had been some visits by curious explorers, but not at all to the degree that your Earth has been visited. The Zenah people had mythology just like you do. In this mythology there were stories of beings from the sky. They always understood that these myths had a grain of truth within them. They always hoped that the myths referred to people from other planets, but they did not have the passion and the desire to really pursue it further.

You will also find that the Zenah people did not have a lot of science fiction. They had little imagination regarding life on other worlds. This was pretty much due to their mythology. Your mythology is complete with half-human, half-animal figures, winged figures, figures that can perform extraordinary feats. Through that mythology your imagination has been nurtured and allowed to grow. The mythology of the Zenah people was a bit more generic; it was not filled with extraordinary tales. It was filled with occurrences more akin to folk mythology. Their myths were more down-to-earth, yet mysterious. Their imagination was not able to be developed the way yours has. Please understand that a planet's mythology is intimately connnected to its ability to imagine!

We knew that because of these traits of Zenah, certain methods of contact would not be appropriate. For instance, one of the methods to disseminate information about contact on Earth is through writers who write fantasy and science fiction. This would not work on Zenah because of their lack of imagination. As a whole, their written language is not as versatile as yours are on Earth. Through Earth languages you are able to express exponential ideas. Their language was a bit more two-dimensional and not as fluid, which limited the imagination.

It was decided after study that we would begin with the telepaths of the society. Every society has telepaths, which are like a built-in mechanism that helps the society to maintain its spiritual connections. This is, for the most part, a universal idea. For some planets, telepaths have to be in hiding. For others, they can be open among the people.

On Zenah the telepaths were often in several different positions. Some of them were in the planetary religious structure as priests. They would "channel" messages from God to the congregation. That is a very simplistic form of channeling and expression, but this allowed these telepaths to sharpen their skills. What they were really doing is channeling the higher self of the mass consciousness to the congregation.

The Zenah people are also very connected to their land. They have not separated themselves from their planet as you have. Thus, many of the telepaths would channel information from the nature energies themselves. Those were the two primary uses for telepathy in the Zenah culture.

The first step for myself and several other telepaths who were present was to establish a telepathic link-up. We first did this with the Zenah priests when they were in prayer with each other. You see, they would often conduct prayer meetings with each other. We first contacted them in one of these meetings. In all honesty, this shocked the pants off them. They were really only used to channeling from one main source — the higher self of the mass consciousness of their planet, or what they called God.

At first they thought it was an aberration of the priest/channel. It was humorous, we will say. They thought he was so aberrated that they proceeded to conduct all sorts of rituals with him. One ritual was to keep him immersed in a certain bath for about 48 hours. They thought there was some type of neuroelectrical imbalance that was allowing him to channel the messages in a distorted way. These baths, which were naturally detoxifying, actually made him a clearer vehicle. After a 48-hour bath, a fast, and prayers being said over him, the messages from us began to come in even more strongly!

We would like to tell you the content of the messages. I was the primary message sender. We keep it very simple and very generic at first. The primary theme of the messages were: "We are of God. You do not know us. We live in another place. We have found out about you, and we want to become friends." The messages were almost childlike and very nonthreatening.

They do not have the belief in good and evil like you do on Earth. Therefore, they did not believe that this could be coming from a demonic source. Whenever confusing messages were given, they believed the messages were either coming from the source as claimed, or they happened because of an aberration of the channel.

The messages continued daily over a period of two to three weeks. At first I sent messages that were very short. Finally, we allowed them to ask questions. By this time most of the priests had accepted that they truly were making contact with other beings. Please understand that there was no deification here. They did not think of us as gods. We were "other creations" of God to them. They did not question that.

In the next stage we explained to these priests that they had to be used as a lens. We told them that if they could refract our energy into their mass consciousness, the contact would be able to occur. If our ships appeared in their sky, some people would see them but would never see them for what they really were. They would translate them into their own symbology — for instance, they would look like Zenah's own flying machines. We didn't want to open contact that

47

way. We wanted to work from the inside out so that these priests could refract energy into the mass consciousness, which would then cause a shift in the mass consciousness so that the vibrational resonance between us would become compatible. Then we could simply appear at some point without a lot of fuss. They don't have the resistance that you on Earth do.

After we studied their religious practices and rituals, we incorporated their rituals into an exercise that we wanted them to do which would help the mass consciousness accept contact. We didn't want the priests to do anything too alien in order to introduce us to their people, so we cloaked the processes we wanted them to do in their own ritual.

We asked them to perform these rituals for three consecutive nights. Then, we asked them to stop doing the rituals for three consecutive nights. Then we asked them to do the rituals again for three consecutive nights. Then we asked them to stop for three consecutive nights. And then we asked them to perform the rituals for the final time for three consecutive nights once again.

This planet is unique (and this is very convenient). They do not have time zones on their planet. Their day is equivalent to approximately 30 of your hours. Thus the hours would be measured by "hour 1," "hour 2," and so forth. What is also interesting is that nearly everyone sleeps at the same time. Because of this, they all have a strong mass conscious connection.

The priests were asked before the sleep time to perform a certain type of ritual complete with chants and movements and visualizations. This was correlated with the time when everyone was just going to bed. What this did was open a rift in the mass consciousness. These priests were thus acting like a lens and refracting energy into the mass consciousness at an angle by which it could be accepted.

After the three consecutive nights of ritual by the priests (repeated three times), there was a noticeable difference in the planetary energy. The abilities of the people to imagine had magnified. Their consciousness was a lot less rigid than it had been before. The planet on a mass level began to dream. This is where it becomes exciting!

They dreamt about us!

Part of the ritual we had given the priests was a vibrational chant

48

attuned to the vibrations of the first-contact team. When the Zenahs were exposed to these vibrations, the vibrations acted like a magnet that would draw their astral bodies to us. So they visited us in their sleep state. They began to see that they were having synchronous dreams. When they visited us in the sleep state, we made a point to allow them to see as much of the ship as possible so they could gain a perspective of a vehicle in space and the people who occupy it. We also made it a point for them to be exposed to the different species on board.

Of course, as they began to discover that they were synchronously dreaming, they looked forward to each of these nights with much joy. So it began to be a celebration. They didn't realize necessarily that it was a first-contact program, but they did know for the first time that someone was out there.

On the final night we felt we needed to punch a hole through the layers of their consciousness. They projected themselves astrally to us, and through the use of the rituals that the priests had been doing, each of these individuals woke up in the astral state and found themselves with us. It took on a different level of reality than they had ever experienced. The awakening lasted only about 20 seconds. In that awakening they saw us and they experienced reentering their bodies. There was no break in the consciousness from the unconscious to the conscious mind. That was the final night.

After that we evaluated their acceptance of this; it was very high. We knew then that face to face contact could now begin.

The first thing we did (myself and two others) was to appear to the priests at a prearranged time. We appeared at the bedtime of the planet. We performed the rituals with the priests in person instead of through the channeling process. This acclimated the mass consciousness to our physical presence. Again the priests acted like a lens. They were able to refract our energy at the angle the mass consciousness could accept it. Our physical presence began to be a factor in all of this.

I must tell you that when we appeared, the looks on the faces of the priests was worth the whole experience! By agreement, we came via molecular transportation. (You would call it "beaming in.") We did not land our ship. We beamed into an adjoining room and then knocked on the door and walked in. That way it wouldn't seem too alien. When we walked in, they were nervous, excited, incredulous. They nearly fell over each other to welcome us!

We kept the visitation very short to keep from overloading them. We went there to do the ritual and then we departed. We did this for three consecutive nights. We did not allow any type of extended communication because of the overload factor. They were very grateful because they sensed the care that we took in acclimating them according to their own customs. Then we called in a secondary first-contact team of about 50,000 to handle the mass acclimation.

To summarize the process, there were three consecutive nights of physical contact with the priests, three consecutive nights of nothing and following that, the secondary first-contact team acclimation began. This was a very rapid contact case. In this particular case, the momentum was very great. To break that momentum would have done a disservice to the contact program.

For three consecutive days after that, the secondary contact team made themselves visible in areas of their world where there were a lot of people. The priests had been communicating with the population (through telecommunication systems), so they were prepared. This was handled in a very organized, nonthreatening way. So for three consecutive days the ships were seen in the sky. Some of the ships landed or the contact teams beamed in and made their presence known. They didn't really communicate for any extensive period of time, but they were there long enough for the reality of the situation to sink in. That is pretty much where my personal part of phase 1 of this contact program ended. I will be going back. The secondary contact teams took over.

In phase 1 we did not form solid friendships with the priests. This was deliberate. We were very warm and formed bonds, but we did not form the type of friendships that happen through long periods of interaction. This specifically was to prevent a focus on particular individuals and to open them to contact from many different species. I will be going back, and they know this. It is then that we will form a more solid friendship.

You see, each contact program is designed specifically for the belief systems of the planet. Your planet provides quite a challenging experience for those of us involved in a first-contact program.

Let's say you are on the ship and you are getting ready for this contact. What are you going through?

I am very excited. There is no fear. They are certainly not a violent people. My desire was to make sure that we communicated as clearly as possible so that we would not break the momentum of the contact program.

Who were the other members of the contact team?

There was a young being from Essassani and there was another species represented that we've never spoken about.

Why was an Essassani part of the contact team? Isn't there a radical difference in vibration between the Zenah society and the Essassani?

There is a radical difference, but we wanted to have a species represented who very clearly pulls you to center when you interact with them. This was so the priests could stay focused in their excitement. The priests had seen us all, as they were telepathically connected with us, so they were prepared for the three different species. The Zenah species basically came into being through the unification of several "shipwrecked" species on that planet. Thus their society is built on the unification of those who are different.

The Zenahs were excited and very curious. It was during the final brief meeting when we first allowed the Zenahs to touch us physically. We didn't allow it at first because the Zenahs had to believe in our physical existence totally *before* they could touch us. Even though they saw us physically, they didn't necessarily believe totally in our physical existence.

Did you speak with the Zenahs verbally through language at all?

Mostly it was telepathic. A linguist later spoke in their language to them, which was a great honor for them. The priests were capable of telepathic focus, which allowed for our initial telepathic connection. Most of the secondary contact personnel were trained in a rudimentary use of the Zenah language to interact with the general public.

This story has demonstrated that the dreamstate of the planet being contacted is one of the most essential places for the first dissemination of energy to occur. It is the vehicle that allows for your acceptance of the energy in the conscious state. This is why more and more people on Earth are now reporting dreams of contact. Yet, your planet still invalidates those dreams. Until they are validated within yourselves and until you realize that perhaps these things are really happening, you are not really going to find the solid contact outside of your dream reality. You must first accept it in the dreamstate, for that is the most easily accessed point. If you cannot accept it in your dream realities, you will *not* be able to accept it in your waking reality. That is the one point we would like to stress more than any other in this story.

Contact is coming in many forms — and it does not at all adhere to what your conscious mind defines as contact. The biggest stumbling block in bringing about contact on your planet is your conscious mind. The conscious mind is continually invalidating contact in its many forms. The conscious mind is continually demanding more proof (according to its own terms), even when it logically knows that proof cannot happen! We cannot comply with that because, from the broader perspective of contact programs, we know what works and what doesn't. And we are not about to engage in activities that, in our past experience, do not serve you.

So why not have a massive dreamstate contact so that people will start correlating their dreams?

We will not do this with Earth as we did with the Zenah because the interpretation of your dreamstate reality will always adhere to your belief systems. You have so many different belief systems on Earth that dreamstate contact would always be interpreted differently. For instance, a good portion of your planet would believe that they were being attacked by demons. A good portion of your planet will believe that it is the rapture and they are going to be lifted off. Massive dreamstate contact on Earth would not promote planetary unification and the acceptance in the mass consciousness of the true nature of the contact. It will keep you divided. We cannot promote that type of massive contact program for Earth when we know for certain how it would turn out.

Why are you concerned about unilaterally contacting everyone on the planet and having everyone respond in the same way? Why not just focus on the people for whom contact is acceptable?

We must use the dynamics of your planet. For example, look for a moment at the birth of Christ as being one big contact program. He was someone with a message. This did not spread throughout your planet so that there was a complete understanding of the truth of it. It was warped and caused much pain, suffering and killing. There are still people who would fight against what Christianity or Islam represents. That tells you right there how contact would be accepted. That is your paradigm.

But why contact someone in order for the news to spread? Why not just contact them for that person only?

There are certain laws of evolution. We've seen time and time again in our studies that unless a planet begins achieving a global identity, they will not successfully merge into the galactic community. This past experience has been quite reliable. This is true of societies who are a lot less resistant than you. Your society presents one of the greatest challenges to a first-contact team. It must be handled with great care. Contact on an individual level – one by one – will not create the most advantageous scenario for Earth regarding its eventual integration into the galactic community.

Each person will interpret the contact differently – either according to their religious beliefs or through their own fear. It is only going to cause more chaos right now in Earth's level of development.

We do things on an individual level anyway, though.

You *deny* your mass-consciousness connections. Until you stop doing that, what you suggest will not be beneficial.

For so long human nature has been individualistic. Why not tailor a contact program to meet that criterion?

Listen to this statement closely: You have chosen individualism *not* as a true expression of who you are, but as a *denial* of who you are. That denial does not represent a belief system; it represents your fear. Unification (instead of individualism) has frightened your people greatly.

The Zeta Reticuli abduction situation is forcing you to look at your own mass-consciousness connections. [See the book, *Visitors from Within.*] The Zetas fear individuality. You fear unification and the loss of individuality. In their own way, the Zeta Reticuli are helping

53

you to eventually create the inevitable contact. They are getting you to face that which you are denying, which is your own unification.

Isn't it ironic that you are examining the complexities of contact philosophy with people on a planet who haven't yet experienced overt contact?

Not really. You are one of the few societies with whom we discuss this. This is because eventually *you* will be conducting your own contact programs with other worlds. If your contact program goes smoothly on Earth, then humans will be adept as first-contact liaisons as well. For those of you who are impatient to get this over with, that is something to look forward to! ∇

5
The Common Ground

"If we want to begin to function on [the extraterrestrials'] level, we have to begin to BE on their level . . . if a big part of their existance is in the realm of nonlocal mind — consciousness — then we have to begin to look at that."

—Steven M. Greer M.D.
International Director of CSETI
1993 International UFO Congress

Our television and movie screens have been filled with the image of a huge mothership hovering over a clearing filled with scientists in the wilderness of Wyoming. We have been fed a steady diet of cute little aliens being protected by human children from an evil government. Through our fiction, it seems that we have tried every angle in order to make peace with a situation that surely will cause friction when it has to be confronted in the future. How will we deal with aliens when we finally acknowledge their presence? How will we initiate a dialog with them?

In order to cultivate solid and meaningful interpersonal relationships with extraterrestrials, we will need to learn an entirely new way of communicating. We cannot rely on our own Earth languages as the sole means of interspecies communication. Instead, we are going to have to become more flexible — build a bridge between two worlds upon which a common ground can be created. Here, on this common ground, the metamorphosis of our consciousness will begin.

Δ Δ Δ

Sasha: The type of contact your planet is preparing for is not so much that the extraterrestrials are going to come and land. We are not going to enter your reality in that way. That is not what you are

55

preparing for. You are preparing to enter the extraterrestrial reality — or, more specifically, for you and us to enter a common reality.

Often in the past you've heard us and other entities talk about how a common ground must be created. It is there on that common ground that we will meet. That common ground can be likened to an energetic frequency.

Each contact program with different planets must be conducted according to the specific ideologies of the planet. On Earth, you have such a wide range of ideologies, such a melting pot of emotional flavors, that you are really going to need to reach to us rather than have us reach to you. Please do not think that this implies that you have to go through some very dramatic means to do so, such as building huge radio telescopes or spaceships; that is not what we are talking about. What we are talking about is that you will begin to deal with certain things in your reality that you haven't dealt with for thousands of years. As you do this, you will vibrationally begin entering that common ground where we are waiting for you. It is a matter of perspective. From our point of view, we are both traveling to a common ground.

The whole idea of going out to the desert, sitting in your lawn chairs, looking at the stars and then having a ship land where you can meet the ETs and shake hands is a wonderful idea in fantasy. There is nothing wrong with that, because that fantasy will prepare you for the reality. But that is not the type of contact that will occur. Rather, what is going to happen is as follows.

To illustrate this, we are going to use the analogy of Magellan again. This is a very flexible analogy and very useful for our purposes. Let us restate it. Magellan once landed on a very primitive island. He anchored his very tall ship out in the sea and rowed to shore. The natives he met had been exposed only to their own canoes, so the rowboats landing on the shore were not an alien idea. The natives could therefore perceive them for what they were. However, that tall masted ship anchored at sea was something very alien to the natives' reality. They literally could not perceive it.

After Magellan worked with the shamans or holy people of the society, the shamans were eventually able to energetically assist the

56

community to see the ship that was anchored there all along. It was simply a matter of introducing new concepts, ideas, and a new vibrational expansiveness into their own framework of reality.

What has been happening for Earth is that many of us (such as myself and many others) have been like Magellan and the shaman. We've been introducing to you new ideas and reality frameworks so that you will expand your vibrational reality to such a point that *you will begin seeing what has been here all along.* We want to make it clear that you are preparing for a reality shift, so that what was there all along will finally be perceived by you.

There are several ways to prepare for that, including utilizing the steps that Germane outlined in the chapter "Preparing for Contact." By no means is that the only way to prepare. Each person will have his or her own ways of doing so. The steps Germane gave are an ideal scenario. If everyone were to carry out those steps, then you would be preparing very quickly and with the least amount of effort.

So contact is occurring now? We don't remember it, so as we shift are we going to start remembering what has already been occurring, and will it flow from the past to the future much more gracefully than we can presently imagine?

Absolutely. Reality always flows. When you turn on the hot water faucet, the hot water seldom starts flowing immediately. You have cold, then lukewarm, then hot water. All reality blends like that. You don't have cold to hot, though sometimes it is perceived that way.

So, it is not so much that we are going to gradually start meeting you more frequently, or anything like that. It is rather that your own perceptions of reality are going to begin shifting and changing to the point where extraterrestrial contact will start to be recognized as having been there all along. This is already happening.

To some degree, the abduction phenomenon is demonstrating that what we are saying is true. There are indications that the abduction phenomenon began in the 1930s and 1940s. But then, those experiences were hardly ever remembered. The barrier between your conscious and unconscious mind was much greater then. But suddenly, in the last ten, twenty, or thirty years the barrier is beginning to lessen. These memories that could once be compartmentalized within you can no longer maintain an identity separate from your whole awareness.

This is why there are so many awakenings of contact memories now. It is not because they are increasing; it is not because the ETs are telling you it is time to remember. It is simply because your consciousness is expanding and able to encompass the new realities, which *include* extraterrestrial contact. This is the nature of the evolution of human consciousness and the evolution of the brain itself. What you are going through right now is not only a massive neurochemical change, but an electromagnetic change in the brain that will allow you to perceive greater views of reality. *That* is how contact is going to occur.

A parallel to this change is the impending revelation of UFO material that has been kept under wraps for fifty years. You may wonder what the connection is between expanding consciousness and why ET information has been kept under wraps for so long.

Here is the connection: When someone experiences a trauma, the mind will often fragment itself (even to the extent of multiple personality) in order to protect the ego from pain and disorientation. If you look at an individual's structure of consciousness as a microcosm of the consciousness of the human race, you find that when an alien idea (no pun intended!) is introduced into the mass consciousness, something similar may happen. If the new idea is so alien that it presents a threat to the status quo, the energy of the mass consciousness will begin fragmenting and compartmentalizing the information from other parts of itself, just like trauma can do in the an individual's consciousness.

Let's look at the 1947 crash of a saucer in Roswell, New Mexico. The mass consciousness of your planet (and not to mention the individual consciousness of most people) could not yet handle the frequency of that type of reality shift. It simply was not compatible with your reality paradigm at the time.

Over the last fifty years, these secrets have increasingly bubbled to the surface; this can be likened to repressed memory in contactees. Same idea. You are now expanding your mass consciousness (just like the individual's consciousness is expanding), and as the mass consciousness expands it is able to encompass new reality paradigms.

58

This allows what was once compartmentalized to begin very slowly to integrate into the whole. This leads to spontaneous flashes of repressed memory.

Your species has never admitted an interconnectedness with each other to the point that you could begin logging your inner experiences and comparing notes. Other species, like the Zenah, have done this fairly easily. In comparing your memories you could begin to construct a truth. Instead, you are bringing these memories of contact to the surface through the uncovering of suppressed material. The energetic dynamic is exactly the same. You are now releasing the memory of something that was traumatic to the whole in such a way that it will begin to be accepted and integrated by the mass.

So, you have two forces working here: One is the gradual expansion of both mass consciousness and individual consciousness to begin encompassing new ideas and releasing old traumas or secrets. Secondly, as this happens, your reality paradigm will naturally begin expanding. You will then be able to perceive new ideas, which will allow you to perceive those of us who have been here all along. These two forces of transformation are working hand in hand.

You are now going to find more and more information of a revelatory nature coming to the surface. The speed at which that information bubbles to the surface will be an indication to you of how fast you are awakening to the contact that is already there.

From your Pleiadian point of view, what type of contact with us do you value? What excites you more — physical, face-to-face contact or nonphysical contact?

The most exciting type of contact for us is one that makes an emotional connection with you. This would encompass physical contact and dreamstate contact. It really depends on the individual's contact scenario. We value emotional connection, by which we mean the emotional connection of equals. We are not excited about an emotional connection with a species who sees themselves as children and us as their parents; that is a relationship of need.

So in your world you value your energetic relationships as much as your physical relationships? This includes relationships with things (as well as people) such as your food and your land?

Absolutely. That is the most important.

And you value your dreamstate contact with other beings highly as well?

Yes! It is all equal. Various types of contacts with humans are equal as well, whether they are physical or nonphysical. If we were experiencing an emotional connection with a human, then it is something that tremendously excites us. Do not misunderstand this to mean that when we encounter a human who is needy, it does not excite us. It is a different type of excitement. The needy person presents a challenge.

So your dreamstate contact with a human can be as exciting (or more exciting) as physical contact?

Yes. Imagine living in a wheelchair your whole life, then one day you can walk. When we meet you in your dreamstate, you act like that person getting out of the wheelchair. Watching that is tremendously invigorating.

So that is one factor that determines why physical contact is often not that common.

Yes. There are also obstacles, so to speak, to the emotional connections that can occur during physical contact right now with humans.

What are some other ways to enable human perception to reach a common ground with the ETs?

We have spoken a bit about electronic devices that entrain your brain-wave states. There are many of these devices on your planet now. Some of their names are: MC^2, Inner Quest, Mind's Eye, and there are several clinical models. These entrain your brain for the theta and alpha brain wave states. This allows you to have more conscious control over entering those states. When you entrain your brain in such a way, it is like exercising your muscles. As these muscles are exercised and you are able to trigger those theta brain-wave realities at will, then you are that much closer to entering our reality.

Let us give you a disclaimer, however: In no way are we implying that you should exchange a theta reality for your normal waking beta reality. We are not talking about that type of denial. We are simply talking about an expansion of what you already have now.

So traditional meditational techniques, if taken seriously, would achieve the same thing?

Yes. There are many ways you can use to enter the common ground that lies between us.

How about simply having fun?

That will do it, too. Having fun being fully centered and not denying who you are (which includes the pain inside) will also get you to that common ground. That is why Germane included as one of the steps "confronting fear." When you confront your fear you are dealing with your own pain, which actually allows you to become more fully who you are. This then allows you to enter that common ground as well.

Literally, whatever device you feel attracted to will serve to help you reach that common ground. At this point you are all standing on one of those moving sidewalks. You keep thinking that you have to run to get to the other end. But even if you stand still, you are going to get there eventually.

Sasha, how are you personally going to help introduce us to the galactic community?

I will be assisting you the way I am doing now — through the channeling process and the introduction of new concepts. Also, I will be continuing my dreamstate interactions with many of you. It is my understanding, as I read the energy now, that beginning in May of 1993 myself and other Pleiadians will be turning up the volume, shall we say. Dreamstate contact will increase and become more intense.

In an ideal situation, what types of places would you like to make first contact physically?

First of all, it does depend on the situation. Let us give you some examples. The type of land in which we prefer to appear physically is usually at higher altitudes. That is more comfortable for us. Also, we prefer rural areas. Those are first choices. That would include Arizona, New Mexico, Colorado, Utah, and any area where the M-band noise and psychic pollution is not as strong. We are not likely to land at Fenway Park in Boston! This is simply a reflection of our preferences.

What kind of people would you ideally like to be there?

61

We would prefer people who represent a cross section of your world.

Would you prefer to appear to people who have gathered specifically for the contact, or those who are gathered for other reasons?

There is no difference. If they sense us, they will gather themselves no matter what. We don't have to gather them. Making an appointment with us for a meeting makes sense in your reality, but not in ours. In our reality we do not make appointments. We don't bind the future like that. Our reality does not even hold that concept. In our reality, we live in the moment and the moment brings us to synchronous meeting places.

Let us give you some examples of areas that are being considered for eventual landing sites. The reasons for these choices are more symbolic than otherwise. One is Hiroshima, Japan. One would be anywhere between Roswell and Albuquerque, New Mexico. Another would be Switzerland, most certainly, because of its historic neutrality, its altitude, and its most famous contact case [the Billy Meier contact case]! These are symbolic landing sites that have more meaning for you than for us. We would choose sites on your planet that have had much war and are now at peace. That is why Hiroshima might be chosen. We are speaking hypothetically here; we are not saying that there is any plan in motion for these landings. This is more to demonstrate how a site would be chosen for its symbolism to you.

Imagine for a moment, Sasha, that you are an Earth person and you want to establish contact with extraterrestrials. How would you go about doing this? What would be your motivations?

My motivations would be to experience more of creation, to learn, grow, and discover the undiscovered. I assume your reasons are the same. It is an insatiable curiosity that all sentient beings have been blessed with.

And how would I, if I were human, go about establishing this contact? I would probably go about it the same way that you have. Maybe at first I would try to build radio telescopes and try to get them to hear me — not realizing that they've heard me all along. Then maybe I would go out into the desert with flashlights and flash them in the sky to get their attention. Maybe I would then try to reach them on an inner level through channels. Then maybe I would, in frustration, give it all up for a while until I finally realized that the process of preparing for contact is not an external process, but an *internal* one. Once I really learned that on an inner level, I would put down the flashlight and the telescope and work on that inner level. Then I would see and feel profoundly the changes that would happen. That would be my validation that I am heading toward that meeting ground. I can only answer that question from my own perspective!

Another channeled extraterrestrial consciousness once said that the ETs are going to show up in our reality when we finally get so excited and absorbed in our own reality that we don't even notice that they land.

That is a very good point! That is one of the reasons why we were attracted to the Zenah. Their evolution got them to a point where they suddenly began to be very excited about who they were. That attracted us greatly. Many of the positive contacts you have with ETs are happening because we are reaching out to very excited individuals — individuals who don't care if they make contact, but who are simply excited about the universe within them. We are attracted to those who are excited. If you are unexcited and in need, we are not all that attracted.

So someone who is beating themselves up for lack of ET contact is not one who will attract contact!

Exactly. When you have a rich inner life, you will attract us more strongly than you could ever do right now by looking in the sky instead of within.

The most significant goal right now is getting to the common ground. To us, it is the only goal that matters. When the goal is bringing about the contact no matter what, you are going to experience frustration and betrayal. That goal is too rigidly focused. Allow the goal instead to be an evolution of the self, and this will lead you to the common ground every time. Everything else will take care of itself. ∇

6

Unconscious Resistance

"Extraordinary encounters appear to be the gateway to a radical, biologically-based transformation of the human personality."
— Kenneth Ring, Ph.D.
The Omega Project

The human psyche defends itself against confusing or threatening stimuli. This is one way that we can maintain order in a seemingly chaotic universe. Each minute, our brains are bombarded by an overwhelming array of stimuli. In order to process this stimuli, our brain first chooses the stimuli that we are familiar with — tastes, smells, shapes, and sounds, as an example — and then it relays this information to our conscious and subconscious minds. Any stimulus that is foreign to our brain's conditioning is often filed away for later internal processing and categorization.

So what happens when a totally new set of stimuli is introduced to our perceptions? The brain tries to process it according to its familiar reality paradigm. When it fails to process it satisfactorily, the brain relegates this new data to the subconscious for later analysis. Often these new perceptions we are exposed to are never brought to the attention of our conscious minds. After all, our conscious minds already have enough to do.

It stands to reason, then, that when a human is exposed to a multidimensional phenomenon (such as a confrontation with ET energy), the brain is ill-equipped to handle such a foreign experience. Instead of feeding our conscious mind the perceptual data, it does its job very well by filing the experience away — thus depriving us of new experiences in perception. This type of data processing has gone on for millennia with a myriad of new experiences that escape detection by the conscious mind. This will continue for millennia unless we challenge the brain to learn new ways of processing perceptual data that will open up our latent talents in multidimensional perception.

The brain is very adept at hiding confusing perceptual data, and it is also very ruthless at continuing to protect us from this nonconforming stimuli. The brain uses the human emotions as a protective device against confusing stimuli — in the form of unexplained fears and unconscious resistances. These unpleasant emotional experiences are like red flags that stop us from probing deeper into the recesses of our minds where new and exciting experiences in perception lie.

In this chapter Sasha addresses some of these unconscious resistances humans carry that stop us from probing deeper. She encourages us to look beyond our frightening and uncomfortable emotions so that we can begin to discover the wealth of new experiences lying just beyond the conscious mind.

Δ Δ Δ

Sasha: We would like to discuss the idea of the unconscious resistance that most of humanity faces regarding the issue of extraterrestrial contact.

About 95% of all humans have unconscious resistance toward the idea of extraterrestrial contact. This means that even though on the conscious level they may be very excited and have no fear whatsoever about contact, underneath there is some latent fear most likely connected to humanity's past ET contacts.

The first idea we would like to talk about is the ancient extraterrestrial contacts between humans and various groups of ETs. When we say "ancient," we are talking about long before recorded history. We are talking about the transitional period between what you know as Neanderthal and Homo sapiens. This was quite a long period of time. During this period, there was a significant amount of ET interaction with these early humans in the form of genetic experiments and improvements.

We understand that this book is not about that topic, so we are going to make it very simple and brief. Simply put, for thousands of years during this transitional time, early man was routinely abducted.

During these abductions, there were many experiments and alterations made on the cellular level and it was often a very fearful experience for early humans. As you can imagine, a fear such as this in a young species would create a fear in its collective consciousness as it evolved further into sentience.

From the time of early man, then, humankind has carried this dread about the outcome of ET contact. It is not as if these memories can be accessed consciously by human beings at this time. Accessing them is very rare, though some people have been known to do so. This primitive fear acts more like a knee-jerk response in the consciousness of the human. When humans perceive the ET energy approaching them, some unconsciously erect a barrier between themselves and the ET.

We will address later in this discourse how that barrier can be relinquished and healed. For now, suffice it to say, the barrier is there, whether conscious or unconscious. In some people the barrier is strong; in others it is weak. It depends upon the individual. Nevertheless, it is there to some degree.

This brings us to the present day. As you know, there are abductions (your word, not ours) being carried out today by the species you have termed the Zeta Reticuli. [See the book *Visitors from Within*.] These abductions are for the purpose of information gathering, genetic experimentation, and sometimes genetic alteration. So not only are they triggering the primitive fears of humans (from the ancient abductions), but they are also generating new trauma that the human needs to confront. The idea of being abducted is such a great terror to humans on the unconscious level that it often requires a great deal of will to confront and heal it. These two levels, present trauma and past trauma together trigger the knee-jerk responses of fear and avoidance.

Whether or not a human is being abducted in present time is irrelevant to this fear issue. The collective human consciousness (which is always unified) will register this fear whether or not an individual is having the contact/abduction. This is one of many collective fears in the consciousness of humankind.

Thus when a present-day abductee experiences even benevolent contact, the trauma is often retriggered, preventing a neutral or

67

positive meaning for the contact. Instead, the individual enters a perpetual loop of emotional stress. That creates, of course, a barrier to contact.

So you see, on that level you are dealing with an intricate tapestry of negative emotions beginning at the very dawn of man's contact with ETs. This is no small matter. It must be healed to be released.

So this encoded fear from ancient days is very much a species fear and not so much an individual fear?

Absolutely, yes. One of the greatest species fears that you have is of the darkness, and being captured. Yes, some of these fears relate to your primitive memories of being part of the food chain. However, some of them also relate to the time when humans were taken at night by so-called superior beings.

In our society, we don't deal well with species awareness. We don't know how to process and heal species emotion. There are no rituals to help us, as there used to be. Because we are so highly individualistic, we like to deny that species awareness even exists.

You have not lost this species awareness because of your individuality. You've lost this because you have lost, in a sense, your belief in magic. The more indigenous cultures on your planet like the Native Americans, Aborigines, etc., have not lost the sense of magic and mystery. They have incorporated mysticism into their lives to allow their lives to make sense. This provides a balance between thought and emotion, and between physical and nonphysical reality. That balance is missing from the Western mind, and that has caused you to retreat into your individuality. Becoming individualistic is not a response to any positive evolutionary process; it is more of a *denial* of who you truly are.

Primitive man responded to stimuli in a way similar to the stories you have heard about the hundredth-monkey effect, where a certain group of monkeys on one island learned a skill, and that skill was transferred through the morphogenetic field to another group of monkeys in a distant place. When you have a consciousness that is not ego-centered, there is much more unification between the individuals of the species. Ideas are communicated more readily. So you see, it is the ego that keeps you individualized. It is the ego that has allowed you to feel alone within a highly populated world.

68

So facing that ancient fear we experienced as a species also triggers a fear of losing our individuality, since to feel the fear we have to merge back into the species mass consciousness.

Yes. To feel the fear fully to heal yourself, you must lose your individuality. This happens whether you go backward into the past or forward into the future with the Zeta Reticuli. No matter where you turn, you must be willing to relinquish the denial of who you are, relinquish the individuality, confront the fear, and then literally create an entirely new construct of consciousness. That construct you create will be much more receptive to true extraterrestrial contact.

You have mentioned releasing our individuality. Is that really what you mean?

Let us put it this way: You will need to release your rigid concept of individuality as well as the fearful need to force expressions of that individuality.

So in terms of the Zeta Reticuli, they are dealing with us not as individuals but as a species. Could this be why there is so much miscommunication regarding the abductions by the egocentric personality of the abductee?

Yes. It is not just the Zeta Reticuli. Other species who have had contact with humans have found it is very rare that their message and the meaning for the contact is ever understood fully. It is always misinterpreted and distorted.

Your species presents one of the biggest challenges for any first-contact team. Your species is like the wild card of the galaxy! (We don't in any way mean that derogatorily.)

Let us continue. There is another very important unconscious resistance toward contact that we would like to address. This unconscious resistance has to do with the **parental archetype.**

As you know, on your planet you have had hierarchical structures that have delegated authority throughout history. You have perceived reality through the eyes of hierarchy. There has always been someone above you; there has always been someone below you. We guarantee you that even the most evolved person on your planet still perceives reality through the eyes of hierarchy.

69

You as humans might view your government as being a notch above you in the hierarchy. Or you might view your priests, gurus, or your favorite writers and thinkers as being above you on the hierarchy. Therefore this constant perpetuation of the belief in hierarchy has allowed you to alienate yourself from your extraterrestrial cousins. This is because in order to fit us into your framework of reality, you've had to perceive us through the eyes of a hierarchy. Most of the time, you've not put us below you. (Perhaps this is because you see us as having more technology than you.) So the most obvious place to put us, according to your model of reality, is above you.

Please remember this: *This role that you have assigned to us does not in any way, shape or form represent our true reality.* You have assigned us a role similar to the role that you assign your parents. When you are growing up as a child your parents are your world. They are all you know and they represent your most important role models. In your interactions with ETs as a child species thousands of years ago, you assigned us that same parental archetype role. We were the caretakers. We were the primary caregivers. We were the ones who, you thought, brought the rain. We were the ones who you thought were gods. You expected punishment and acceptance from us. When we left the planet there were periods of great depression and sadness because there was a feeling of being abandoned by the primary caregiver. When we would return, there would be the joy of unification. But underneath that joy, there would always be the anger of abandonment.

This is the same process that occurs through childhood development for humans as individuals. When your mother does not come when you cry, you feel abandoned. When she does come, you feel the joy of reunification, but that anger at being abandoned is *never* released. You grow to adulthood carrying that anger and subtly expressing it in whatever way you can throughout your life. Your childhood development as humans exactly parallels your development as a child species. The ETs who were your forefathers represent that parental archetype.

When you feel our energy approaching you, such as in a contact scenario, it triggers all of those ancient emotions you felt when you saw ETs as your major parental figures. When contact happens you feel, on one level, a great relief that we have returned at last and will

70

make it all better. Whether or not this is a conscious belief, it is a response that we sense in your emotional bodies. As you know with your logical minds, we are *not* going to make everything okay. We cannot take responsibility for your reality. But the part of you that is still the child species still has that automatic response. *It is that response that still keeps us at arms length.* Until you process the fear of abandonment and the willingness to give your power over to an outside authority figure to take care of you, it is going to be very difficult for us to achieve any type of successful open contact program. We will no longer be your gods, as you have heard us say many times. We will no longer take responsibility for your pain.

To heal this pain within you, it would be much more difficult to go back through time and attempt to tap into the species pain. Instead this pain can be healed right here, right now, in your daily life. Each and every one of you have your own pain from your own process of growing from child to adolescent to adult. One of the main issues being worked on among your people now is the healing of the inner child. You do not have to go into the species childhood to heal the relationship with extraterrestrials. As you go back and heal your own inner child and your own relationship to your parents in *this* life it will have a domino effect. You will then heal your relationship to the parental archetype—which includes the ETs. There is much work being done on your planet now to heal the inner child. Just about everyone involved in consciousness expansion is dealing with this issue. Even people who have no conscious awareness of dealing with any of these issues are having these issues triggered and are moving through healings.

This is why you sense us so close and yet so far. As we have discussed already, we are here. We have been here all along, yet you cannot perceive us. We will not reach out openly until you have reached out openly to us. You have not yet done this because this relationship with the parental archetype is not yet healed. It is coming up for healing now, and it will be healed very soon to the point where we can both reach out toward each other.

So as we view an ET, we automatically project a parental image upon them which stands in between ourselves and the ET?

That is correct.

We are attempting to interact with the illusionary image. It is an artificial construct. It has very little depth.

Yes! You are interacting with a ghost image that does *not* represent who we really are.

One of the characteristics of a child's consciousness when it deifies a parent is the emergence of various hypnotic phenomena. These children are perfect trance subjects. They go into trance and see their parents through a form of hypnosis that is apart from the actual experience of the parents themselves. Is this where we are, also? In a sense, do we hallucinate during our contacts with ETs so that we project onto them what we need them to be to support our own inner programming?

Yes. That is correct. You have made a lot of progress as a species. Thousands of years ago you did openly deify ETs on the conscious level. You are not doing it consciously now, for the most part. That growth has occurred on the conscious level. However, on the unconscious level there is still much more deification than you realize. As you know, there is a lot of ET communication literature that still mystifies and deifies extraterrestrials. This is done through the presentation of hierarchies or through the perpetuation of the idea of good and perfect ETs who are going to save you. It is still the same idea. *That does not represent reality!*

As you know, in simple traditional psychology, one of the most crucial steps to personal empowerment is demystification. It means taking the idolized figure off the pedestal and setting him down beside you. When the demystification process begins, the internal healing process also begins. That is when a *true* rapport between the once-deified being and the human can then begin. That is exactly what is going to happen with the ET phenomenon. Once the ETs are taken off their pedestal, demystified, and no longer idolized, a true rapport and a balanced relationship can begin. It cannot begin before that. Until then, humans will always see a ghost image which is a two-dimensional projection upon the screen of their consciousness that does not represent the greater reality of the experience.

This is a great challenge, yes. However, it certainly is one that can be mastered. Once it is all said and done and healed, the trance will be broken. You will gain a view of reality you cannot yet imagine.

This new view will more closely approximate the reality that the greater You perceives as real.

So what other resistances to contact might there be? There is a great resistance unconsciously toward the idea of the **dissolution of your mythology**. Your mythology on Earth (be it Greek, Sumerian, Mayan, whatever) has been the cornerstone and foundation of the way you view reality. You do not necessarily consciously believe that Osiris was cut up in pieces and was put back together by Isis. Few consciously believe that. However, mythological stories such as that represent archetypal energy accepted by the mass consciousness of your species, and that raw energy is used to explain reality. We understand this to be a very esoteric concept, so let us give you an analogy.

Imagine that you have a bunch of stone tablets that depict the Osiris/Isis story. As your society grows and develops, let's say you've lost the ability to read those tablets—but you *know* they are important. So instead of reading them and using the knowledge, you use the tablets to build a floor or wall of a temple. They then become part of the structure and framework of your reality even though you can no longer read them and understand the original information.

As a result, your mythology has become woven so tightly into the very fabric of who you are that you can no longer even see that it is woven. All you see are the structures you've built based upon the mythology.

Some humans unconsciously fear that totally embracing ET beings will crumble the mythology that humankind has built. This means that not only will the mythological stories possibly be proven false, but the very structures built from those stories will crumble as well. The human consciousness at times sees this as a total dissolution of everything it knows to be true. That idea, in and of itself, is extremely threatening. This is not a fear on the individual level. This is a fear on the species level that creates great resistance against accepting beings who might cause humans to change, alter, or destroy their mythology.

There is a way around this. It is not really feasible to go back into your past and dig up the mythology and heal it that way. However, you do need to create a stepping stone or bridge to the future. This

73

means creating a new, contemporary mythology and using it in a different way than mythology has ever been used.

Let us return to the idea of the absence of mythology in Western scientific culture. Look at the indigenous peoples on Earth such as the Aborigines and the Native Americans; mythology still plays a very important role. That mythology, because it is alive and allowed to change and transform, allows a fluidity of change within the indigenous cultures that you may not necessarily see on the surface. Western culture, because of its desire to remove mythology from daily life, has created a void and a rigidity, which makes any change in mythological structures very difficult. If Western man is willing and able to create a different type of contemporary mythology (perhaps through the use of archetypes), then mythology will be reawakened and the ancient energy locked within the structures you've built will once again come alive and, in a sense, animate itself. Once this happens, the fluidity will begin to be reestablished in those structures and you can then move from the past to the present and thus to the future.

This is beginning to happen already to some degree through the resurgence of the men's movement and the interest in Native American cultures. That is the way you are going to move from rigidity to fluidity. Once this ancient structure that has been built upon your mythology is again infused and animated and the contemporary mythology begins changing, it is then that the doorway to ET contact is truly opened.

So you are saying that mythology provides flexibility, like water within a sponge?

Yes.

So this ties in with our model that mythology came from an incomplete and immature relationship with our ET forefathers. You are saying we cannot reestablish contact with our relatives without mythology?

Recognize that before ETs were visiting your planet, primitive humans had mythology. It was an *indigenous* mythology.

So the primitive humans saw the ETs through their own mythology?

Yes.

74

Do you, as a Pleiadian, initially perceive other species through your own mythology? Is this natural to all species? Is this what brings about the most fulfilling and enriching contact, when the mythologies engage? Do mythologies draw you together?

One question at a time! Recognize that it is the same as asking, "What comes first, the chicken or the egg?" One can look at history and say that mythology came first and then the ETs slid into the mythological picture. Another can say that the ETs came first and mythology was created around their interactions. Well, both and neither are true. They came together. They complement each other. All of reality is a reflection of the archetypal world within. Everything is simply a reflection of what is within. Should humans choose to view the ETs as their mythical characters coming to life, then that animates their inner mythology. We will simply say, neither the "chicken" nor the "egg" came first, but were born from each other and coexist alongside each other.

In other talks you have said that when one species contacts another species for the first time, they send archetypes to each other. Are not archetypes myths?

Archetypes are the seeds from which mythology springs. An archetype is the First Cause, shall we say.

I think that to understand this concept we are going to have to broaden our concept of what mythology is. Mythology is not just a story that is passed down; it exists within the mass consciousness.

Yes. There are many levels to mythology. But the first and foremost thing — the seed that germinates into mythology — is the archetype. You are seeing a resurgence now of exploring archetypes such as the Female Warrior.

We as a species have rejected our old mythology but have not yet formed a new one. So in regard to the ETs, we have not sent the appropriate mythology out to greet them?

Yes, in a sense that is true. Also, you cannot recognize or decode the archetype/mythology that we are sending to greet *you*. To some degree the word "mythology" is a bit misleading. We simply want to stress that when we refer to mythology we are not talking about stories. We are talking about the *primordial energy* from which the stories spring. The common ground is when both of us enter that primordial stream. It is then that we speak the same language. Do you understand what we mean by this?

Yes. But what is that language?

How do you want us to describe it? Since neither of us speak it together, how shall we describe it? **The common ground is the language of shared perceptions.**

There are some studies in perception where one animal is raised only around spheres. Another animal is raised only around squares. Their perceptions become limited. When they are brought together they do not have a shared view of reality. To some degree that is what you and the ETs are dealing with. Your perceptions differ, and therefore the fundamental language between you differs as well. Once you train yourselves to perceive the same shapes, so to speak, you then enter a common ground where communication can occur.

There is one more thing we would like to address regarding the unconscious resistance that humans face regarding ET contact. This is in the area of **addictions**. Humans, for the most part, have an addiction to their view of reality. The continuing fulfillment of this addiction gives you the illusion of completeness. But the drive to fill the addiction comes from a feeling of tremendous aloneness.

A most obvious addiction is the addiction to religious thought. Humans become very threatened when their view of reality must be forced to change by accepting a new concept. Often they would rather remain safe than risk changing the way they view reality. Obviously, open contact with ETs will mean that religious viewpoints will need to become less rigid. To those who have deep addictions to religious thought, this will be a very painful and difficult adjustment. Some people have unconscious theological addictions whereby they have a certain view of the universe (heaven and hell, for instance) that provides them comfort. Any concept threatening that view will trigger an absolute and total defense. As the ET contact approaches and humans begin feeling that their views of reality are threatened, you may actually find more religious fervor — whether on a group level or individual level. It will be a challenge.

For whom?

Certainly for those desiring to relinquish their theological addictions. Because, as you know, people attempting to break an addiction do not even know when they are acting out the addictive behavior.

So what is the connection between ET contact and religious addiction?

Those who have certain addictions to religious thought have a set package of how the universe is ordered. If an ET comes along, that package might be upset. The neat and tidy hierarchical structure must change. Religious addictive thought does not necessarily conform to logic.

When the ET energy approaches humans who have religious addictive thought, certain things may happen. One is that they will be triggered on the species memory level. The triggered area will be the ancient memories of the ETs as gods — with both the pain and the joy associated with those memories. It will usually be an aversive feeling rather than a joyous one. Humans will not want to deal with that past pain. On another level, as we have discussed, the presence of the ET means that they have to incorporate that ET into their own theological view. In most cases this will be very difficult and humans will need to create a high level of illusion to maintain their addictive beliefs. In either of these cases, psychological stress is imminent.

So if you contact a human, the addictions come up and block the progression of the contact. Interesting. What aspect of ourselves is refusing to be present and hides behind the addiction?

The aspect of you that refuses is that which is terrified of taking 100% responsibility for your reality. That, we would say, is the biggest fear facing mankind. Your interaction with ETs, as you will soon see, will show you that we cannot be controlled or manipulated by your addictions. You have become very used to manipulating each other out of the fear arising out of your own lack of self-responsibility. It will not happen with us. That is terrifying for you.

Are we afraid of accepting the blame for the mess we are in?

You believe that accepting responsibility is the same thing as accepting blame. It is not a matter of blame! It is a matter of simply living in such a way that you always create consciously what you wish to create. It requires that you no longer blame others, either. It has been very easy to blame us for your mess. It is very easy to blame negative ETs for terrorizing you. It is very easy to blame. But it is not easy to claim responsibility. Engaging in the blame game will be the single most powerful deterrent toward your embracing of ET contact.

This time, you are not going to enter the arena of ET contact by being victims of it. You are not going to be the primitive people the gods use as pawns. You have chosen that it won't be that way again. This means that you have to act as equals to them. You cannot be needy or manipulative. Since that has been a way of life for many of you for generations, it is very terrifying.

We will not enable you in your need. We will not give you a false sense of security. And we will certainly not allow ourselves to be manipulated by you. What then? You must learn to be totally self-empowered and treat us the way you would want to be treated yourself. You have not yet been able to do that amongst yourselves.

Please do not misunderstand what we've said as any type of criticism or judgment upon your species. We simply state the facts which we believe most of you would agree with. The power structures on your planet have maintained power through manipulation. This has given a signal to your people that manipulation is the way to achieve power. You are now unlearning that behavior and beginning to teach yourselves what true power really is. When you learn that and your eyes are open, you will see us standing there, where we have been all along. ∇

7

Inside the Contact Experience

"In a universe in which the consciousness of a physicist affects the reality of a subatomic particle ... we can no longer pretend that we are separate from that which we are studying."

— Michael Talbot
The Holographic Universe

Often when we are communicating verbally with someone, we respond to their unconscious body language. We also respond to their other, more subtle forms of communication such as voice tone, eye contact, and speech patterns. Later as we analyze what we've said to the person, we may wonder why we behaved in a certain way or why we didn't say the things we really wanted to say. What we haven't yet realized is that communication occurs on many other levels that are totally separate from our conscious mind and vocal expressions. We often *do* say what we want to say, but we say it through other forms of expression.

If we on Earth find such challenge in our own interpersonal communication, it seems reasonable to assume that interspecies communication with an extraterrestrial will be challenging indeed. How can we establish a true rapport with ETs as well as avoid simple misunderstandings when we cannot even do so with our own mates? This presents probably the most significant challenge to the whole contact experience and it is one challenge that may not ever be triumphed over until we learn about the real nature of the human consciousness.

In this chapter Sasha presents more information on the mechanics of contact, as well as a look at how the extraterrestrials interpret our communications, which are a source of confusion for them. She also addresses how human belief systems adversely affect communication with nonterrestrial beings.

Δ Δ Δ

Sasha: We would like to speak more to you about brain-wave states and how those states are important to the contact experience. As before, we are going to use your models of brain-wave states because our models are somewhat different.

You have defined four major brain-wave states in your sciences, as we have previously stated. The **beta** state is the one you exist in your normal daily awake time when you are engaged in tasks or having conversation. This is the brain wave that locks you into physical reality. It is also the brain wave where your ego is the most active in keeping you focused in this reality.

Alpha is the state you enter when you are daydreaming, lightly meditating, driving, or doing any type of automatic behavior where your mentality is not engaged. Most of you spend a good portion of your day in alpha when you are not actually concentrating on a task.

Then you have **delta**. This state is the one you enter when you are deeply asleep. It is the state where many of your dream interactions occur. Most of these dream interactions are not necessarily remembered when you awaken.

Then, there is the **theta** state. It is here we are going to focus much of this discussion. The theta state is the most elusive for humans. Yet at the same time, it is a pivotal point for the expansion of consciousness into other realms. It plays a major role in shaping the elasticity of your consciousness. The theta state occurs either in very deep meditation or in the state between waking and sleeping. It occurs when you are falling asleep and experiencing what is called hypnogogic visions — spontaneous internal stimuli which seem like lucid dreams just before you fall into true sleep. This usually lasts for only a short period of time. Theta then gives way to delta, then you are asleep.

If we were to tell you that contact experiences are most likely to occur in a particular brain-wave state, it would be theta. Theta and delta are separated enough from the conscious mind that you may or may not remember the encounters you have when your brain has switched to that frequency. Right now in your world there are many devices that are used to entrain your brain to use the theta state more efficiently [see Chapter 5]. These devices will allow you to achieve a more elastic consciousness. They also help you to strengthen your lucid dreaming abilities and teach you how to enter the theta state at will.

Theoretically, if you can train yourself to enter theta at will, you will be training yourself to enter the common ground that the ETs can enter as well. This is one place where contact can occur. The kind of contact many of you envision is not going to happen in your beta/awake state. This is because the beta brain wave is a very narrowly focused frequency (like on a radio dial). It is so narrowly focused that other levels of consciousness (be they extraterrestrial or interdimensional) cannot slip into that frequency for any length of time. Beta is a very focused frequency; it was set up deliberately to keep your ego grounded in physical reality. It is a gift of the third-density reality you exist within.

As your consciousness is now learning to expand, you are going to find that on a daily basis the percentage of time you spend in beta will be reduced. The percentage of time you spend in alpha is going to increase. This may result in many of you feeling more spacy than usual. Eventually, as your percentage of alpha rises, the percentage of theta will rise also. (Alpha is a bridge to theta). It is in the alpha (but mostly in the theta) where other levels of consciousness can communicate with you. Your perception of reality has very much to do with the brain-wave states that you experience on a day-to-day basis.

We have discussed the idea of allowing your reality to become more elastic. It becomes elastic, literally, by the change in your brain-wave frequency. As this frequency changes, your perceptions of reality become more elastic, and then, obviously, what you create becomes much more limitless.

Is it true that as we are going to sleep, we go from beta to alpha and then to theta?

Yes, in a sense. However, it is really much more multidimensional than that. All the brain-wave emissions exist simultaneously. When you are awake, beta is dominant. But even when you are awake, alpha and theta are active — it is just that they are at a lower level. When you are asleep, delta is dominant, but the other brain waves are still active on a lower level.

As a side note, let us give you some interesting information. From our point of view, while this channel [Lyssa] is channeling, beta, alpha, and theta all peak. Delta increases as well. For the channel, this allows her consciousness to become more elastic. You have seen that over the last eight years more and more people have become channels. Why? There are lots of reasons. But one reason is because of the exercise that channeling provides for the brain. This eventually allows the brain capacity to expand and affects a person's ability to perceive a more elastic reality. As you become more elastic, your perceptions of reality change. As they change, your ability to actually have ET contact changes as well.

So the question then becomes, do all of you have to learn to channel in order to benefit from this? No. However, the hundredth-monkey effect is in play here, too. One of the reasons why there are so many channels is that, through their own increase in brain capacity, they are providing a way for the critical mass to be reached so your brain capacities as a whole can then take a leap.

It is a wonderful beginning to envision contact to be like *Star Trek*. Your imaginings of Captain Picard getting out of his ship and shaking hands with an alien is a great exercise to move you toward real contact. It has to start somewhere. If you can't imagine it, you can't create it. The more your perceptions of reality expand, the more you can imagine the possibilities.

Do not assume that contact will occur in your waking reality with someone walking up to you and shaking hands. If you assume that is the only way that valid contact can happen, your consciousness will become rigid instead of elastic. You will be limited in your perceptions and actually wait longer for open contact to happen.

We would like you to use the model of the brain-wave states to begin to grasp what happens to you when you have contact. We were asked the question, "Sasha, would you give an example of a contact a Pleiadian has had with a human who was awake?" We briefly addressed this is Chapter 2 but would like to expand upon it.

We have already told you about a woman who lived in a very large metropolitan area of your planet. We will call her Janice. She was working alone very late in her office. She had a very strong connection with Pleiadian energy. Her own soul had agreed to have a contact that particular night.

A female Pleiadian walked into her office. You would think that if a female Pleiadian (who is not too alien to you, relatively speaking) walked into your office at night, you would see her for what she really is. However, this is what really happened.

Janice was sitting at her desk. As the Pleiadian approached her, the energy field of the ET hit her first. So even before she looked up, she sensed the energy. Upon sensing that energy, her brain-wave state began to shift. Janice looked up, not because she heard a sound but because she suddenly felt very disoriented as her brain waves shifted very rapidly. The first image Janice saw when she looked up was that of a humanoid (the actual female Pleiadian) dressed in a man's business suit. This was an incongruous vision. We're not talking about a feminine-styled business suit that female executives wear. Instead, this was a straight, boxy business suit that was obviously too big for the female Pleiadian. This incongruous image was the only way that Janice could make sense of what was coming toward her. Once Janice's ego registered the strangeness of the experience, her consciousness entered what we would call dreamtime—theta consciousness. Her ego was no longer in control. This does not mean that the interaction itself was a dream, no. The interaction itself simply did not adhere to the rules of your *physical* reality, which are organized by the ego. The ego was not the orchestrator of this experience, so the rules changed.

Janice had her interaction with the Pleiadian, which consisted of energy exchange and discussion. The next thing that Janice's ego was aware of was waking up on the couch in her office. She woke up and thought, "The last thing I remember was sitting at my desk and feeling strange. Ah, I must have felt dizzy, laid down, and fallen asleep." She never explored the amount of time she had lost or the remnants of incongruous memory she had. Instead, she simply attributed it to dream images. Situations like this happen more times than you realize.

These compartmentalized contacts happen like this simply because of the great difference in your brain-wave capacity and the brain waves of the aliens contacting you. The only place that they can meet you is on the common ground. For most people, they must disengage from physical reality in order to get to that common ground.

So a logical question would be, "Well, what about Billy Meier? Why did he have face-to-face, awake contacts?" [The Meier case is a well-documented contact case of encounters between Edward "Billy" Meier and several Pleiadian beings, the most notable a female named "Semjase."] Meier and others like him who have had physical contact are part of a minority of humans whose brain-wave constructs are somewhat different. He is wired differently, so to speak. He was able to achieve a dual perception both in alpha and theta, which allowed his body to move and maintain an identity with the world. At the same time, he had an interaction with someone from another species.

Often, Meier's encounters were not physical in the way he recounts them. But that is the only way he could translate the experience into words. Sometimes his contacts were the same type that many of you have — which occur either during sleep or meditation or in an altered state. He is wired in such a way that alpha and theta are the primary expressions for him. Your primary expressions are beta and alpha.

Many of you may have heard rumors that he is unstable. We are not going to validate those rumors, but we will say that Meier does not relate to the world through the same type of ego that most of you do. He does not relate to the world through a beta consciousness, but through an alpha/theta consciousness. Therefore, his perceptions of reality are different. When he comes into contact with individuals who have more anchored egos (beta consciousness), his ego construct is so alien that it may be interpreted as emotional problems. This doesn't mean he is more evolved. He is simply one of the groundbreakers who has chosen to be a pioneer into a new level of consciousness. As you know, pioneers are often the ones who are ostracized.

Think about what we've said as an example. There are other contactees on Earth who have had experiences with ETs in the same way Billy Meier has. Those people are wired differently from the majority of humans on Earth. *All* of you are wired differently from each other, so your contacts are going to be different as well. If you

84

compare your contacts with those of another and strive for what they have, you will be striving in vain.

We were talking about the critical mass effect before. Meier is one of the people (among other contactees) who are helping to change the elasticity of the human consciousness. This is one of the services he has chosen. But please do not feel that if your contacts are not like Meier's, something is wrong.

$$\Delta \quad \Delta \quad \Delta$$

Sasha: We would like to discuss the ego. It is true that all beings who have physical bodies have an ego mechanism of some sort. The Pleiadians have an ego mechanism as well. The purpose of this ego may be different for each being. The purpose for mine would be mainly to act as an anchor that always draws me back when I need an orientation in physical reality. You will find that the Pleiadian ego is somewhat more elastic and flexible than the human ego.

We would like to give you a deeper understanding of how your egos may respond to contact. There is a meditation we would like to suggest for you that will introduce some ET energy in a very subtle way. If you do this several times, it will help adjust you to the energy of the common ground.

Some of you may be aware of the information we are about to give you. The being called Sasha, myself, is a future incarnation for this channel [Lyssa]. This is one of the reasons why our connection is so strong — in some ways (don't take this too literally) our egos overlap. There are shared aspects of our egos. It is in the overlap of our egos that we find the common ground between us. You are going to find that in terms of one-on-one ET contact, the most common situation is that you will attract a future self (ET, or future Earth) who will be one of the first to contact you. Because you share an overlapped ego with your future self, the communication can be fairly smooth.

Let us refer back to the story of Janice. The Pleiadian who came into her office was a future self of Janice. In the past, Janice had been very resistant to contact. This is one of the reasons why she had to enter an altered state where her own psychological defense mechanisms blocked out a good portion of the contact. Recognize that within about 95% of the contacts between humans and ETs, it

85

is not the ET who is blocking the human's memory of the experience, though it may look that way. Your own human ego is blocking the memory as a natural defense mechanism and also as a byproduct of your compartmentalized consciousness. Because of this compartmentalization, the mechanisms of your consciousness cannot handle the circuitry necessary for complete and full memory of the experience.

Let's say that your subconscious mind is receiving ET communication. Because of the compartmentalization, it has no way to pass that information on to the conscious mind. You view this as a form of amnesia. If the memory ever leaks to your conscious mind, it takes the form of memory fragments that cannot be traced back in time, and are then dismissed. There is no way yet for you to totally remember the contact and express the memory through your conscious mind. Since your reality is dominated by beta consciousness (or the conscious mind), *you automatically assume that no contact is valid unless it happens when you are conscious.* But there is a whole lot more going on!

As the boundaries between your levels of consciousness begin disintegrating, the memories will begin to resurface. No one is putting memory constraints on you. It is simply that you are not yet wired to remember. This is changing.

If Janice had not been resisting contact and had been gradually assimilating the energy, what would have happened? Theoretically, the next step would have looked like this: Janice would have first sensed the energy of the approaching ET, then upon looking up and making a connection, she and the ET would be drawn to each other like magnets. Because they are aspects of the same soul, together they would enter the area of the commonly shared ego. This would probably produce disorientation in the following way: Janice would be standing there one moment looking through her own eyes at the Pleiadian. Simultaneously, Janice would be in the body of the Pleiadian looking at herself. Imagine what that would be like! It is much more disorienting than you can possibly imagine. Because of that deanchoring of the ego, the contact would have lasted only a short time. Then, most likely, she would have fallen asleep. However, on waking Janice may have vividly remembered that very experience, but simply attributed it to a dream.

So you see, there are gradations. There are levels of the contact that happen as you get assimilated to the energy. So we are going to give you an exercise whereby you can begin to introduce yourself to the energy of a future ET self. This will open a doorway for you. Practice it, but don't take it too seriously! Relax and enjoy yourself.

Please don't do the exercise while you are reading this. Read the exercise first and then go back and do it. You may do it as often as you wish. When you are ready, make yourself very comfortable.

Preparing for Contact Exercise

Take three very deep breaths. With each breath feel your physical body begin to relax even further. Imagine a golden energy covering your toes. As it covers your toes, you can feel them relax. The gold energy moves up and covers your feet, ankles, and calves. As it does so, you relax even more. The energy then moves from your knees up your thighs to your hips. You begin to relax even more. Then the energy moves from your hips over your torso to your shoulders while you relax even more. The golden energy moves from your shoulders all the way down your arms to the tips of your fingers. You relax even more. The energy moves from your shoulders up your neck and head until your entire body is covered by this golden energy. You feel relaxed and at peace.

Now imagine that around your eyes is a band of electric blue light. This band runs all the way around your head and covers your eyes like a blindfold. Feel the reality of this blue energy around your eyes. Then imagine, almost like a winter hat, a violet cap of energy over the top of your head. Feel the reality of this energy around your head. Continue to notice that with every passing moment your physical body becomes more and more relaxed.

Now imagine that you are in the front room of your home. It is a safe and comfortable place. Imagine that there is a knock at the door. The knock is soft and gentle. Do not walk to the door, but glide to it. It is almost as if you are on wheels. Stand in front of the closed door. From the blue band around your eyes, send a blue beam of light through the door to the entity standing on the other side who also wears a blue band of energy around his/her eyes. You are now connected by this blue energy to the entity on the other side of the door. Allow yourself to feel a sense of familiarity with the being on the other side.

Place the palms of your hands on the door itself. Imagine that the entity on the other side does the same. Through your hands, you both send blue beams of energy to each other. You are now connected not only through the blue band of energy around your head, but through your hands as well.

As you imagine yourself standing there with your hands on the door, close your eyes. Use your will now, in cooperation with the entity, to change the molecular structure of the door. Imagine that the door begins to dissolve. As it dissolves and your eyes are closed, your palms are touching the entity's palms. Feel the pressure of the entity's hands upon yours — the electrical sensation that passes between you. It is very real.

Count to three. Upon three, open your eyes within your visualization. As you do so, give yourself a brief moment of sight as you face the entity. Look directly at the entity, but do not linger. Then deliberately shift your perceptions so that you are that entity looking back at yourself. Then shift back into yourself again and look at the entity. Quickly shift once again so that you are the entity looking at yourself. Do this several more times.

Visualize coming back to your body. Feel the pressure of the hands of the entity against yours. Through your will and the will of the entity, reassemble the door into its original position. This time when the door reappears, it has a small window it did not have before. It is a permanent window that will allow you more of a view into another reality. Take your hands off the door, put them by your side, and take three deep breaths. Open your eyes.

We suggest that you do this exercise at home as often as you feel drawn to do so. This is a brief taste of the exercise. Do not worry about what you feel during it. Do not invalidate it by convincing yourself you have fallen asleep. You have not. Each of you will respond differently. Practice it. It will help you assimilate the energy of any ETs who have already been in contact with you.

Δ Δ Δ

We would like to give you an illustration of what happens, from an alien's point of view, when they interact with a human whose consciousness is compartmentalized. When ETs come into contact with you, they do not perceive a whole integrated being. They instead perceive three levels — the conscious mind, the subconscious, and the unconscious. These levels do not directly communicate with each other. Therefore, the ET must, in a sense, deal with these three separate parts as if they are three separate beings.

To illustrate, the example we give here is a dramatic one. Please do not take offense. Let us say that a Zeta is going to interact with a woman named Mary. This Zeta receives several communications from Mary, which are all on different levels. Mary's **conscious/ego mind** will say, "No! Leave me alone!" She may actually scream this in physical reality.

Mary's **subconscious** (which is where much of your programming and conditioning from childhood is stored) says the following: "Abuse me, because abuse equals love." You have heard about this in traditional psychology. When children are abused from a very young age, they begin to equate abuse with love. So when they grow up, they naturally attract abusive mates or friends. The programming in the subconscious causes one to seek love in the only way it has defined it — through abuse.

The **unconscious** is saying this: "I agree to this interaction. This is for my growth on all levels of my being." The unconscious, in this case, can be equated with the Higher Self.

Thus when the Zeta enters the scene, he is getting three broadcasts all saying different things. (He has a hard enough time with humans in general!) Which broadcast does he pay attention to? Well, he hears the loudest one — the one that overrides the others. It is almost like receiving three different radio stations over your radio. Your attention will automatically be directed to the broadcast you can hear the most clearly. The rest becomes background noise.

The conscious/ego who is shouting, "Leave me alone!" represents the beta brain-wave state. Most ETs cannot enter this place with humans. It is unique to the human species, so they cannot enter that reality. We guarantee you, this is the voice they hear the least. They are not ignoring you. *They simply cannot hear you.*

The voice of the subconscious says, "Abuse me, because abuse equals love." The Zetas don't necessarily know what a human means by "abuse me." So for the Zeta it comes across as, "Do what you want with me. I give myself to you." The Zeta may also be able to tap into Mary's subconscious to the point where he recognizes that Mary thinks she is getting love (abuse = love). So the Zeta thinks he is complying with the human's desire to get love. The Zeta may actually think he is giving love. Remember, the Zetas do not know what love is in the same way you define it. All they can see is that they are giving something to humans that humans think they want. Because Mary equates abuse with love, the Zeta thinks he is giving love. Mary, on that subconscious level, thinks she's *getting* love (because abuse is the only thing she knows), but on the conscious level it translates as abuse. On the unconscious level (which does tend to be the loudest voice), the Zeta hears, "I know I've volunteered to do this. I present myself to you to be of service."

We recognize that for some people this is difficult to digest. The ego panics; it needs to be in control. If you do your research into abductions you will find over and over themes suggesting that from the Zeta's point of view, they don't know why you are fighting. They think you've agreed to it.

We are not going to get into abduction psychology here, for much of it is written in *Visitors from Within*. The important point we want you to see, however, is that there are different messages ETs receive when they attempt contact with you. Every ET who communicates with you gets at least three simultaneous radio stations. This is because of the compartmentalization of your consciousness.

If Mary changes her definition of love on the deepest level of her being and learns to equate love with love (instead of abuse), the whole dynamic must shift. Then Mary will no longer attract abusive situations. If the abduction scenario continues, her point of view about her abductions will take a dramatic turnaround because she will no longer need to create abuse in order to get love. She will no longer feel victimized by the experience. Instead, she may actually look forward to it as an adventure.

This is not just theory. The channel [Lyssa] and Keith have been working with abductees and this has already begun happening.

Therefore, the contact experience will always be defined by the belief patterns in your subconscious. It is here that your belief

90

systems will affect all the contact experiences you have. It is in the subconscious that you store your childhood and past-life pain. This old pain is what forms your belief systems. When these beliefs are changed, the entire contact experience changes with it. This is why emotional processing work is *vital* for humans. That work changes the subconscious belief systems, which in turn changes the quality of your contact experiences. The processing work includes (but is not limited to) inner child work and healing your relationship with the parental archetype. We cannot express to you how profound this is.

Until the pattern of abuse-equals-love is healed within humans, you will not be able to sustain an open relationship of equality with extraterrestrials. You cannot sustain a relationship based on equality with us if you cannot sustain it amongst yourselves. You will always see us as your parents who abuse you. If, for instance, we don't give you the technology you ask for, then we are abusive. Or if we give you the technology, you label us abusive because we give it to one group and not another. You will always see us through the eyes of abuse. Nothing we do will be fair to everyone. Now you can see why there is so much frustration regarding why we contact people, who we contact, and when we are going to contact everyone.

We Pleiadians have had moral dilemmas for most of Earth's recorded history over what we were going to do for you and what we were going to allow you to learn yourself. Those of you who are parents know that these are your daily moral dilemmas. How do you teach someone to be responsible for themselves without giving the impression of authoritativeness? Big challenge. So, we will admit, we have stuck our foot in our mouth throughout history and have made a lot of mistakes (from our point of view) in how we have dealt with past Earth contact.

Through the eyes of a culture whose modus operandi is abuse, anything we do can be construed as abuse. Do you see the dilemma we are in? We must be very, very cautious in dealing with humans.

Once the idea of victimization is relinquished and abuse is no longer part of your identity, you will become self-empowered. (That is Step Seven that Germane gave in Chapter One). As this occurs, a whole new reality dynamic will occur in which your species as a whole becomes stronger than it ever has been. It is then that your contact experiences will shift dramatically. A new dawn will break that will be only the beginning of the adventure that awaits you. ∇

8
Releasing the Pressure

"This is all linked. We are looking at a link with UFOs. We are looking at a link of the thought processes of humanity, the consciousness of mankind itself."

— Colin Andrews
Crop Circle Researcher
One on One on UFOs (Video)

Sasha: In the previous chapters we have talked about the compartmentalization of the human consciousness. We have also discussed how contact can occur within one level of your consciousness while the other levels remain unaware of the contact. In this chapter we would like to address what happens within the human psyche as a whole when memories are compartmentalized — especially memories that have strong emotional charges.

First, let us discuss your traditional psychology. You know that abuse as a child will often cause a fragmented memory of the abusive situations. Some parts of the abuse may be remembered, other parts may not be. However, these unresolved, fragmented memories gather energy or momentum within the human consciousness because they are unrecognized. Eventually, there must be a bleedthrough into your reality that is directly linked to these repressed memories. Often (in the example of abuse) this will take the form of raging behavior or emotional problems that seem to be out of control for the person. That results from the bleedthrough of the unrecognized energy from the memory of the abuse.

We are going to apply that idea to the ET contact phenomenon. If portions of yourself are making contact (for example, the subconscious mind), the conscious mind does not remember the contact because it doesn't happen in its domain. A pressure then begins to build within the deeper levels of consciousness. This energy must somehow bleed off and release the pressure so that psychic pain does not occur.

This bleed-off of the excess energy from these repressed memories happens more frequently than you realize. Emotion is energy in motion. Remember that any repressed energy in a person must be released. It will often come out in the form of emotion.

Humans have a tendency to suppress emotion if they don't understand the cause of it. So then you have a dual repression. You have the repression of the original energy of the experience, and then you repress the attempt to release that represesed energy. This complicates it considerably.

When you have such an intense repression of energy, the energy must come out somehow. Therefore, it comes out in its purely energetic form. This can often take the form of psychic phenomena—what you have called poltergeist activity. Those on your planet who have researched poltergeists know that the poltergeist energy is often associated with an individual or a group of people. Often, the poltergeist energy is associated with children, especially at puberty. (This is, of course, the time when the emotional body is the most confused.)

When this energy of the unrecognized ET contact is not addressed in the human consciousness, one of the ways that it will bleed off into your reality is through the creation of unexplained phenomena such as poltergeist activity. This means that perhaps things will fly through the air, strange noises will be heard, or apparitions will be seen.

Excuse me. You've just described a large percentage of UFO sightings and experiences! Things fly through the air; levitation, strange noises, and apparitions are all part of the phenomenon.

Interesting coincidence, isn't it? You have gotten the point. One of the points is that *you are not experiencing the ET contact phenomenon in its true form.* You are experiencing a bleed-off energy. You are translating it into your reality to make sense of it.

The ETs (for the most part) are not causing things to fly across the room. That is the bleeding off of the energy that you yourself (as the contactee) are channeling. Believe us when we say that the entire contact phenomenon looks *nothing* like you have hypothesized.

So are you going to tell us what it does look like?

I cannot tell you that because, going back to the earlier chapters, I am in my dream and you are in yours. I may say "blue," but you will see "red." Our realities have not yet interfaced enough to the point where what we say is not distorted by you. All we can do is leave clues in your reality and point you in the right direction. This will allow you to take the necessary steps to enter the common ground on which we can meet. It is not that we won't tell you; simply, we are not able to.

We are telling you right now in this communication, but we are having to use creative ways to do so. We are having to use grand analogies and concepts that in your reality are understood. But we will be the first ones to admit that even what we are telling you now is not the whole truth. However, it is the truth as it translates into your reality in the present time. It is close enough that it will open some doors for you and begin to allow your consciousness to become more elastic and your perceptions of reality more limitless.

Let us continue our discussion about the bleed-off of repressed contact energy and emotion through the form of psychic phenomena. Some of your classic poltergeist activity can also be placed in the category of ET contact. Some of the groundbreakers in psychical research have come to the conclusion that poltergeists are not throwing things across the room, either, but that activity is a translation of the repressed energy bleeding off through the human vehicle as it interfaces with the energy of the spirit being. Poltergeist activity is only one symptom of the bleeding off of this energy.

Connected to that is the phenomenon of electrical disturbances. Poltergeist activity is often accompanied by electronic disturbance. However, there is often electronic disturbance around UFO activity that has nothing to do with poltergeists, so please do not think we are attempting to link poltergeist activity with electronic disturbance. It is all a symptom of the same cause.

These bleed-offs of energy into your reality serve a very important purpose. If you pay close enough attention, these paranormal phenomena will remind you of the contacts you have repressed. In a moment we are going to give you a very specific example that will hit close to home for you, Keith.

95

Let us talk briefly about electronic disturbances. As you know, when UFOs are in the vicinity, often there is electrical disturbance — whether it be cars stalling, street lights going on and off, house lights flickering, or power lines glowing. That has become part of the classic symptoms of impending contact. However, these electronic disturbances will often mark when you are having contact, and you may not even be aware of it. Let us say that someone is driving down the street and his car stalls. He turns the key and it won't start. Then the motor suddenly turns on and the person drives away. Sometimes (not always) when the car stalls strangely, for no reason, you have contact that is very real and face to face on the common ground. When your consciousness returns to this time stream and reality, the memory often does not come with you. The only thing you have that can serve as a signpost is the physical manifestation of the car stalling.

Several years ago you [Keith] and the channel [Lyssa] took a trip to Monument Valley. You were driving through reservation land in northern Arizona. There was not a soul on the road that you could see for miles. Yours was the only car. The land was flat, with many strange and wondrous surface features that are seen in northern Arizona. As you were driving, the channel heard a voice in her head say very clearly, "Something is going to happen." Ten seconds later the car stalled. There was no mechanical reason for this. The car rolled to the side of the road and she turned off the ignition.

You both got out, looked under the hood, jiggled some wires, and talked about the implications of this experience. You then got back in the car, turned on the ignition, and drove away as if nothing had happened. The whole time you were logically trying to figure out what happened.

We will tell you what really happened. When you got out of the car, you had a contact with me.

(Just a moment, let us pause. The channel is panicking and causing interference! She is attempting to censor because what we say is frightening to her.)

Your contact with me was very brief. You lost some time, though, about ten to fifteen minutes.

This is an example of how easy and effortless contact can be. It can fit in the flow of your life without your ever knowing consciously that it occurs. This has happened for most of the people on your planet.

What was our reaction to meeting you?

First of all, the contact took place on a level of your being where this type of contact is not surprising. You, Keith, were much more speechless than usual. The channel did most of the communicating. She was very excited, but you were a bit frozen. That is quite all right. You were having your own internal revelations during the experience.

After the experience was finished, you returned to your beta/waking consciousness while you were still standing outside the car. You got back in the car and drove away. There was a feeling that something happened. But the two of you, with your logical minds (and your desire for groundedness) would not ever let it go further.

We cite this example as a very valid example for the reader. We also cite it to benefit both of you, because in channeling this book you are having to face your own compartmentalization. The walls are breaking down. That is why we are now able to tell you this information.

So we ask you, the reader, to think about times in your life that stick out. Has anything mechanically or electronically strange happened? You may not ever gain the conscious memory of the contact, but your conscious mind doesn't rule you anyway, so it doesn't matter. For all of you reading this book, know that your contact is very real. It is a part of you.

Thus, electronic disturbance is one signpost to let you know that something might have happened. Another signpost that can hint that a contact may have happened is unexplained emotions. For instance, some people may have absolutely no interest in the subject of UFOs because it arouses a great fear. That fear may directly result from a confusing contact experience they have had. The only way the memory can get to the surface is through the expression of an incongruous emotion — an emotion that doesn't seem to make sense in that person's life. There may be an intense fear of UFOs or of the sky, for instance.

So the confusion about the emotion is a defensive measure to hide the cause of the emotion?

That is correct. Moreover, some unexplained emotions may be a longing for the stars. Of course, we are not making these statements across the board for everyone. Some individuals have had contact experiences where they have actually been taken on board for a flight and experienced the universe. Once back on Earth, the limitedness on Earth has caused them to long for the stars once again. That is one explanation.

There are other individuals who vehemently reject Earth life and have much anger or resistance toward anything that is grounded or part of society. These unexplained emotions are very important to take note of because they can point to past experiences and emotions that may need to be healed regarding these experiences.

Another signpost is the recognition of missing time. Of course, there has been a lot written about this. Sometimes some of you have been driving and have arrived at your destination much earlier or later than you anticipated. You have brushed it off with logical explanations. But often, these missing-time experiences are in fact what they appear to be — missing time. Missing time is a very good signpost indicating contact experiences. In some of these experiences, you are not removed from the time stream physically, but your brain waves shift into another frequency while your body exists in this physical realm. After the shift, the contact experience occurs, then your brain-wave frequency shifts back into that of the physical realm and your body continues to experience chronological time.

Another signpost pointing to contact (which is a little less tangible) is a sudden and profound insight. For instance, you may be walking down the street or driving, and in an instant there is a body of information downloaded into your conscious mind. This is often information that you've gotten during a contact experience, which, when your conscious mind is relaxed (such as in alpha when you are driving), is able to seep through the barriers and become part of your conscious repertoire of knowledge.

While driving, you generally enter an alpha state, which is much more receptive than beta. When you relax your hold on your ego consciousness, whatever information you have been given in another reality can be downloaded. It then seeps into your conscious mind, where it is sensed as a sudden and profound insight. Where the information comes from is not as important as the information itself. We simply want to state that when information is downloaded like this, it is often in response to a contact you have experienced.

Another indication of contact may be works of science fiction that have been downloaded to a writer. Or it could be visionary art transferred into physical reality through the hands of the artist in a very profound way. These are often experiences that have occurred on the theta level (the common ground) with a nonhuman consciousness, which are then downloaded to the conscious mind in a vulnerable moment.

This brings us to one of the most perplexing enigmas that occurs on Earth right now. At the beginning of this chapter we mentioned the raw psychic energy channeled through humans that may take the form of poltergeist phenomena. If enough humans have ET contact that is being repressed within their consciousness, it *will* affect the mass consciousness of humanity quite strongly. Therefore, the bleed-off of this raw psychic energy attempting to escape an individual's consciousness will enter a realm representative of the mass consciousness. In this realm the psychic energy manifests itself in a way that affects the entire planet. To some degree, this is what your crop circles are.

Though the energy of the crop circles has a nonhuman origin, it is not necessarily that the ET is setting out to draw a specific symbol. Rather, as massive amounts of ET energy are channeled into the mass consciousness (and then into the individual's consciousness) the compartmentalization will cause a shutdown. In this way, the energy must be diverted and expressed in whatever way it can. The nature of human archetypes is what actually translates the ET energy into the symbology seen in the cornfields. The crop circles are some of the first manifestations *in your language* of ET contact. It's just that you have not yet identified the language because of its nonlinear nature. It is deeply symbolic. The crop circles themselves are the physical, tangible expression of this raw psychic energy from the repression of ET contact on Earth. It is like a poltergeist manifestation on a large scale that occurs only because of the repression of the ET energy within the mass consciousness. The crop circles are *not* going to go away.

This does not mean that crop circles are not generated specifically by certain extraterrestrial groups. They are. However, as an overall phenomenon, its capability to manifest in your reality is a byproduct of the compartmentalization of your consciousness and the repression of raw psychic energy. In a sense, the ETs ride the wave of this repressed energy and use it to their advantage in order to make contact.

Why does this occur in Britain?

The poltergeist phenomenon is often localized to areas in the house that have distortions in the time/space continuum. The places on Earth that have the most electromagnetic anomalies (or distortions in the time/space continuum) are the places that attract this phenomenon. Britain has one of the most concentrated areas of time/space distortions. The veils between the dimensions there are thin.

Of course, there are other energized areas on your world, such as the Giza plateau near the pyramids. However, no crops are grown there. The environmental conditions are thus not present to translate the energy into crop circles. However, other anomalies happen on the Giza plateau.

The other areas where crop circles have appeared (Australia, Japan, America, and others) are mostly moveable time/space distortions. That is why a crop circle is likely to appear somewhere only once.

The answers to your questions are all around you. However, by the time the question escapes your lips, you find that you are not asking the right question to get the answer you desire. Everything is here for you to find the answers to your most perplexing questions. Part of the understanding requires that you relinquish the limiting hold that the conscious mind has on the reality of your entire being.

Some of you may now think it is necessary to search your lives to find where you have had strange experiences. That is not necessary. This is not about going into your past to dig up what has once happened. It is more about living in the present. As things happen in the present, become more aware of them now. As you become more aware in the present time, that is going to help to disintegrate the boundaries between the levels of your consciousness. Focusing in the past or future is a sure way to keep the compartments intact.

When you stay focused in the present, compartmentalization cannot maintain itself.

In your present day-to-day life, be sensitive to anomalies. This isn't for the purpose of proof, but simply to have a little fun. Bring back the childlike wonderment of your life by boldly going into the world of the unknown.

Δ Δ Δ

The night this was channeled seemed normal enough. We went to bed about an hour after the session was completed. Lyssa had a growing anxiety as she was trying to fall asleep. She kept sensing the energy of the Zeta Reticuli.

Neither Lyssa nor Keith are aware of any "abduction" experiences with the Zetas. However, they both have had some of the telltale symptoms of Zeta interaction (body markings, a feeling of being drugged while sleeping, and odd changes in the sleeping environment). The night of the above channeling, Keith went to sleep as usual by turning on a fan to provide white noise. Often, this is the only way he can sleep peacefully. However, he awoke some hours later to find the fan had been deliberately *turned off*. This is similar to a strange occurrence the night he awoke to find the blindfold he usually wears placed upside down on his head.

Also on the night of the channeling, Lyssa awoke with a sudden and strong need to go to the bathroom. While stumbling to the bathroom in an intensely groggy state, she strongly felt the presence of the Zeta Reticuli behind the shower door. This caused some panic. As she thought to herself, "I feel them in the shower," the water suddenly began trickling down from the shower head loudly and then stopped. She could do nothing to awaken but remained in that semi-sleep state similar to the theta state that Sasha has described. It was here in this theta state that she perceived quite clearly the extraterrestrial energy.

A few minutes passed. Suddenly, Lyssa came to full consciousness in the bathroom almost as if a veil had been lifted from her conscious mind. She no longer perceived the Zeta energy and went back to bed.

Does this mean that the Zeta energy disappeared? Or could it be that Lyssa could only perceive the energy while in the theta state and once she entered beta, the compartmentalization caused a lack of perception?

Later this same night, the symptoms of contact continued. At exactly 5:15 a.m. we were awakened by our two smoke alarms blaring loudly. There was no smoke, but yet we could not shut them off. Suddenly, without warning, they simply shut off. The next day we had them inspected, only to be told, "There is nothing wrong. It must have been some weird power surge."

Sasha's words rang in our ears: "Electrical disturbances are signposts of contact."

We find synchronicity in the fact that on the night Sasha revealed to us information about a past contact with her, we also had strange experiences during sleep time. Perhaps what Sasha said is true: When we begin getting in touch with our past contacts, the veils begin to be removed. As the veils are removed, we are more able to perceive contacts in present time.

Two weeks later Lyssa was conducting a Japanese tour group throughout Peru. One evening as the group sat in a meeting room high in the Andes on the Urubamba River, Lyssa began explaining about Sasha and expressing that perhaps Sasha would visit Peru while the group was there. As soon as those words were uttered, there was a brief power failure, in the meeting room only. The lights went off for about five seconds.

The group was startled, but the discourse continued. Lyssa then jokingly stated that Sasha has said the words, "Electrical disturbances are signposts of contact," and perhaps this incident was her way of letting the group know she was nearby. Immediately upon making that statement, the lights went off again. This time the group was visibly shaken but excited. Once again, the lights returned after about five seconds. The power disturbance did not happen again during the entire stay in Peru.

Coincidence? These types of subtle anomalies happen every day to almost everyone and we never notice. In fact, we've learned to simply ignore them and label them as more of life's strange, unexplained situations that do not warrant closer examination in our busy lives.

102

These stories represent just a few of the constant stream of unusual experiences to which we are exposed. If you, the reader, examine your own life you will also find these strange, playful, and unusual experiences sandwiched between your normal daily activities.

Should we pay more attention to these experiences? Perhaps so. Even if nothing unusual is happening, tuning in to subtle experiences can only serve to strengthen our perceptive abilities. Perhaps it is time to open the door into the unknown a bit wider. ∇

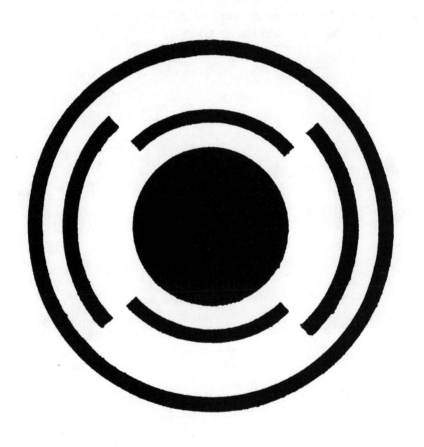

9
Beyond the Conscious

"... the evolutionary fires that are beginning to flicker and dance through our collective psyche may be our wake-up call ... informing us that our true home is elsewhere and we can return there if we wish."
— Michael Talbot
The Holographic Universe

If contact is already happening, what are some of the forms it is taking? Do these contacts adhere to the typical ET contact scenario or are they more of an abstract nature? How can we differentiate "real" contact as opposed to "imaginary"?

In August 1993 one letter, among the many we receive from readers, came to our attention. It seemed to exemplify some of the material we were exploring for this publication. We present an excerpt below.

Bobbie and her husband live in a rural area of Washington state. Her letter was both clear and sincere as she described a profound dream that she had recently:

In my dream it was as though it was actually happening as an everyday occurrence. It was so real. I could feel the emotions, the sense of timing, and hear actual voices. In my dream my husband and I had just gotten home from work as usual. We did the normal routine around the house. I went out and did a few chores, then relaxed for the evening ... I went to my room to listen to tapes and to read. [My husband] watched TV. All of a sudden, the TV program went out and instead, over the air waves on ALL channels came a nearly nightlong message from an extraterrestrial that could speak as male and then gradually change over to female in the tone of voice. My husband came running to my room to tell me to come listen to the TV. (I later discovered the being channeled over radio and computers at the same time.) Anyway, I can only remember bits and pieces of this dream that seemed to go on forever.

There was so much to absorb and remember. The being told of not being in contact with the human race government because of lies that are told to the people. The government coverup was too much for us to understand at this time. The beings were going straight to the people. People should not fear their message of hope. People should not fear the beings having contact with earthlings. The message went on with much I cannot remember. But it said that there are people on earth who are awakening to their heritage of the stars. Some have been aware longer than others, and there are those who "know," but haven't been able to identify with what they know just yet. Many are now awakening to their "birthright" and heritage. People of a lower level of awareness should not fear them, but should seek them out for guidance. The message went on to say no harm would come to those who would guide others in a new awareness. The "forces" would protect them.

One last thing the message revealed was that the people who "know" their true birthright and heritage and who are either tuned in or tuning in to this reality will be "marked by golden." Golden lawns and trees, flower or vegetable gardens, and if there were no lawns, trees, or flowers at their place of residence they [instead] would have golden sidewalks. Finally, well after midnight, the message ended. My husband and I went to bed. I'm thinking in my dream that this is crazy. What is happening?

The next morning (still in my dream), my husband wakes me up yelling from the front room to come and look outside. Everything was the color of "golden" including my fish pond. I ran to the phone to call my best friend. She called me as I was reaching for the phone to call her. The woods around their home was golden and so was her herb garden. She then said the message came over her husband's computer as he was doing some astrology work that evening . . .

Again, in my dream I couldn't get out to go to work. The driveway was packed with people gawking. I had to call my boss and reveal what was happening. As I'm peeking out through the front room window curtains . . . I'm thinking to myself "How am I going to get out of here to go to work?" Neither my husband nor I got to work that day.

The next morning after having the dream, I woke up and tried to make sense of what I had dreamed. I actually thought I was losing my mind.

When I got up to let the dogs outside, I looked out and was even actually very disappointed that everything was green. Every so often I still catch myself casually looking out to see what color everything is. I feel a bit foolish, but it's as though that dream was so real, I can't shake the effects it has had on me. It's as though I'm expecting something to happen. I'm expecting to actually, in reality, be watching TV and hear a message from the galaxy.

Though this dream is unique, its flavor is similar to dozens of letters that we have received over the years. For all of our scientific knowledge, scientists really don't clearly understand why humans dream or what significance dreams hold in the dreamer's life. But one thing is clear. The similarity of dreams regarding positively oriented extraterrestrial contact is profound. Something or someone is sending messages, via the human mind, through dreams. Even if the dream were entirely a product of the human mind, *a message is still being sent from deeper levels of consciousness.* This message is saying that we are not alone and that there is a grander universe to which it is time to awaken.

We have posed some questions to Sasha about Bobbie's experience related above. Her insights continue to open doors . . . but at the same time stimulate more questions.

Δ Δ Δ

Sasha: In the book *Visitors from Within* we told a story about the Betan culture. This civilization was a very rigid one that vehemently denied the reality of ET contact. They denied it not only openly with their conscious minds, but they also denied it within their own consciousness. They shut themselves down to any type of communication from outside sources, whether through telepathy or dreams. So when it was their natural evolutionary time to open up to the next stage (which would be contact with ET civilizations), they found that they did not have the tools to do so. They were frightened and very rigid. They kept themselves quite closed. Thus as contact began, it caused a tremendous amount of friction.

Finally, when the pressure could no longer continue, there was a drastic release. When that happened, the Betans suddenly began experiencing strange phenomena — what you would call poltergeist phenomena — in their waking reality. They also started experiencing

107

together powerful, strange dreams.

The experience of the Betan culture is an example of what happens when a civilization closes itself off from the natural flow of evolution and natural ET contact, which is part of any species development. Upon your Earth now you are not experiencing the rigidity and close-mindedness to the point the Betans did. They are a much more dramatic example. However, you are experiencing a form of rigidity that is unique unto yourselves. For there are portions of your society that very much believe in ET contact and are ready for the next step. There are also portions of your society that are deathly afraid of losing power that they think they have over your world to something "bigger" that they do not understand.

Because of these fractionalized points of view on your world, there is a degree of close-mindedness and rigidity. But as you are entering this very natural stage in a planet's evolution, contact *is* going to come to you. It is going to find a vehicle through which it can slip in, no matter what the vehicle is. For humans on Earth now, the easiest vehicle through which contact can come is through your dreams.

Throughout mankind's history he has always dreamed of contact with other beings, whether they be angels, devas, demons, or messengers from God. This has been a way for the forces to which you are normally closed to channel through you and make their presence known. However, during the last 50 years especially, as the acceleration has begun on Earth and as you are moving into the evolutionary stage where you *must* embrace the reality of other beings outside of yourselves, the pressure is building. Your consciousness *must* begin to perceive these communications that have been coming to you all along. It is as if your stereo amplifier and speakers are suddenly of a much higher quality; by turning up the volume only a little, the message comes through quite clear. It takes a lot of energy to ignore such a message!

Many of you on Earth now are receivers for some of this natural communication coming to you from other realms of consciousness. Those of you who are receiving now are the pioneers. In a way, you are paving the way for those after you; it will be easier for them to accept communication when you have already laid a foundation and paved the way. In a sense, what you are doing also is helping to stretch the limitations of the mass consciousness so that these types of communications do not "blow the circuits."

In regard to the dream that Bobbie had, we would say that she is one such person among many who is a natural receiver for information. The dream that she had (among the others that she's had) was a very real, deliberate, and literal communication.

We've spoken about the different levels of your consciousness and how they can be accessed by your brain-wave states. So in that sense, there is an alpha reality that parallels your beta reality on a moment-to-moment basis. There is a theta reality that parallels alpha and beta. And there is a delta reality that parallels theta, alpha, and beta realities. You, from any given moment in your waking consciousness, cannot necessarily access all these different reality flows. If you could, then you would to some degree be disoriented about which reality you are grounded in. However, some of you at times have accessed these simultaneous reality streams. Let us give you an example.

Sometimes when you are about to fall asleep, you will suddenly find yourself in a reality or scenario or conversation with someone in your hypnogogic state (lucid state), which seems as if your conscious mind has tuned into a scenario already in progress. If you were jolted awake, it may not yet have been concluded, as if entering these other reality streams is like entering a room where there is a scene already in progress and you become a part of it. This is happening on the deeper levels of the human consciousness. Your conscious (beta) reality is not the only stream. You have other levels of reality, other experiences, simultaneously. Sometimes you can slip into these other "rooms" for a momentary peek.

The dream that Bobbie had was an experience where she slipped into one of these "rooms" during her sleep state. She is fortunate because she has remembered such a large portion of the experience. We will say that most people have these experiences all the time. They are being taught by beings on these other levels of consciousness. They are having communication and interchanging ideas. However, when they awaken, most people do not remember. What is unique in this case is Bobbie's detailed recall. This is indicative of how you as humans are beginning to change.

We've said previously in this book that you are going to begin to

109

notice that as you start remembering more about what happens on other levels of your consciousness, you are going to be getting closer to a more open contact that can be recognized by the conscious mind. This is because the boundaries are beginning to dissolve between the levels of your consciousness.

The reality that Bobbie entered in her dream was one that could accept extraterrestrial communication through the most convenient vehicle possible (your televisions and computers). These are two current communication devices that can very easily receive communication from ET sources. In your beta waking reality, your consciousness is still fragmented to the point where communication through that medium would be very difficult for you to perceive. This is because your conscious mind is given the job of selectively disallowing certain perceptions to reach your inner being. These types of communications must be given to you on the level at which they will affect you from the *inside out* rather than from the outside in. This is why Bobbie's communication occurred in the dream state.

The night that she had this experience was a night when communication was given to thousands of people on Earth. If there was a way to survey everyone on your world and compare their dreams on that night (provided they remembered them), you would find a very high correlation of dreams that could be interpreted similarly to the one Bobbie had. It was one of the evenings where communication was very deliberately given to you.

Has ET communication ever been deliberately given in our beta waking state through television and computers?

Yes, it has. It has not been done on a mass scale, because very few remember it. For instance, if it were given to one hundred people, perhaps one out of one hundred would perceive an anomaly through their TV or computer. They wouldn't be able to discern the communication. One in a thousand would be able to actually discern a communication. They may distort it, but still get its gist. The odds are not now very favorable for communication through television and computers in your waking beta state. However, in your alpha, theta, and delta state, communications in those parallel realities are much easier to filter through.

What exactly happens when you attempt to communicate through the

110

TV in our beta waking state? What is the response, and is the response uniform?

The response is very similar to the story told about Magellan. If you remember, the natives could not see Magellan's tall masted ship. When it appeared, they could not see it for what it actually was. They interpreted it according to the only guidelines they had — their own little boats. The same is true for communication through the computer. When it comes through, by most people it will do so in a way that is not even perceived. Or it may be manifested and interpreted as a computer glitch, unexpected and unexplained.

So the communication is screened out after it starts?

The message itself carries a vibration. People will sense the vibration before the message is even fully transmitted.

I've always thought that you ETs are just trying too hard. When in Rome, do as the Romans do. Do you desire to communicate to the masses, yes or no? This is not a trick question!

It is not a yes-or-no question! There is a big difference between desiring communication and actually doing it. Do we desire it? Yes.

It's not a trick question, Sasha. Relax. If one of us desires to communicate to the masses, we go to an advertising agency because they know how to get to the conscious and subconscious minds of the masses. Why not do something along those lines? Would it work?

It has already begun! Recognize that all the advertisements with an ET theme that you have on your world (like Bud Lite, etc.) are not being done by us. Instead, it is you sensing our energy and trying to make sense of it. You are trying to convey the message in your own language. So you are receiving the communication, but you are not receiving it verbatim. You are not receiving it in our pure language and intention. You are translating our messages through your reality screen.

Think of it as a big cookie cutter between our reality and yours. Everything that enters your reality from us has to first pass through the cookie cutter. Its shape is changed when it does so. There is nothing either of us can do about that.

Back to the Magellan idea. We can conceive of your craft. We can conceive of its technological capabilities.

111

In a very limited sense.

Yes, but we can begin to conceive of it. We are a big jump ahead of those natives trying to see Magellan's ship. Our people have already seen craft!

A few people in your society have broken through the veil, yes.

We have crafts that have crashed here! Our own people are studying them. We've seen bodies. I am not disagreeing with you, but I'm trying to draw out more deeper responses. What is the big deal?

Your question seems to imply that you think someone is withholding from you, either us or your government. Recognize that your government's withholding this information merely reflects the very readiness of your mass consciousness. It is not your government holding these things from you. It is your mass consciousness using your government as a tool to hold these things from you.

When the natives "saw" the ship and screened it out, was it the ship itself they couldn't conceive of? Or was it the implications of the information? Do we screen out your craft because we cannot conceive of the shape? Or is it that we cannot conceive of, grasp, and accept the implications of your presence?

It is the implications. If Magellan had drawn a two-dimensional figure of his masted ship on a piece of paper (not telling the natives what it was), they would have seen the image but would not have known what it was. They wouldn't have screened it out. It is the image itself in combination with its implications. It is the image combined with the knowledge that in order to see the image, your very belief systems must be shattered. *That* is what causes the screening. Your egos will protect your belief systems at all costs.

Your governments are the representation of your mass ego. Your mass ego, then, will screen out anything that threatens its own belief systems. That is why the mass ego holds all of the "secret" knowledge.

So what are you going to do about it?

Me personally?

Yes, you and the others. What are you going to do about it?

Each of us has our own agenda. Myself personally, I will simply continue to follow my excitement. For now, my excitement is not so much in showing you the physical structure of a ship, but in helping you to break down your belief systems. I do this by communicating through this channel, as well as communicating with many of you in the dream state. To me, it is much more beneficial to break down the old foundations before you build new ones.

You are talking as if humans have never seen spacecraft. We have, and on a regular basis. Reports come in that large amounts of people have seen them from Mexico City to Russia.

Recognize that as far as the contact scenario is concerned, you are not all operating as a bunch of individuals. You, to us, are a mass consciousness. You are a planetary species. You are *not* individuals, though you have not yet recognized yourselves as a planetary species. As your population grows, the required number of people needed to reach critical mass, and thus change a belief system, increases. So even if you have a sighting in a football field and one hundred people see it, one hundred is not very much in your mass consciousness. Recognize that most of us are not aiming to have you see us visually. Your population as a whole will not see us until your *internal* structures change. Your internal reality creates your external reality.

Perhaps it is our own deficiency in communicating with you. We have been talking about this for so long, yet we still receive questions like, "How can I go out in a field and see a UFO?" Sometimes we think we are not communicating clearly when you keep asking those types of questions.

Okay, so compromise a little. Don't throw away the message you want to give to us. Hold it in reserve. If I see something exciting, I want to bring my friends to see it, too. That is what we do here on Earth. When it comes to UFOs, that is what we are doing. It is simple. It is within our belief system. So why not work with that belief system? Entertain us! It is what we enjoy.

Your civilization has been entertained and used by ET craft and their occupants for millennia. Perhaps you cannot see the bird's-eye view. From our point of view, that type of display is the last thing that should be done.

Why?

Look what has happened to your planet after thousands of years of

ET contact.

But it is the way you do it!

No, it isn't. Your planet is very unique. In a sense, you are a planet-wide orphanage. You have not been afforded the natural development of a species — especially a species that has been seeded. In most solar systems, when a planetary system is seeded by an older race, it is their *right* to guidance. The new race has a *right to know its heritage.* This has been kept from you. Because of this, much planet wide dysfunction has occurred. We will not do anything that will add to that dysfunction. You may not see how certain methodologies may add to the dysfunction, but we have thousands of years of experience behind our knowledge. This experience clearly reveals to us what we need to do and what we should not do.

Well, I think it is going to be a long time before we can ever communicate on this clearly to agree or disagree. I don't hear you responding directly to the idea I put forth.

From our point of view, you are not asking a question that makes sense. Perhaps we are lost in the translation.

We are doing this session for a book. One of the themes running through the book is the problem and difficulties of contact. It is a given that you desire contact with us. It is a given that there has been difficulty in contact. So the idea I am putting forth is to simply do what we would do initially. This won't cover the primary contact, but it'll begin to break down certain structures.

We are already doing that. We are doing it in the dream state (and other levels of consciousness) and in the waking state where applicable.

You know we humans like to fly. We like air shows. We stand on the ground and gasp at aerial phenomena. Can you specifically respond to the idea of doing that with us? Wouldn't that build a bridge?

Perhaps you are not hearing us. **When we do this, most of you do not perceive us.**

There are too many cases where we have perceived you.

Your channel sitting before you (who has been exposed to the reality of ETs her whole life), along with two other individuals saw an extraterrestrial craft in their full waking consciousness. They

114

could not perceive it for what it was. They had to perceive it as a very cartoonlike airplane instead! Doesn't this tell you something?

How many seconds in duration was this?

The actual sighting was several minutes.

This says that we need practice at perceiving these things.

You are still under the assumption that every contact your conscious mind is aware of is the only time you've been given practice! You are given more opportunities to see our craft than you consciously realize.

I totally agree with you. I would be giving this same speech to an audience. But part of the problem is how you are defining the term "you." This book is only for the most narrowly defined "you" — the conscious mind.

When I address those aspects just outside your conscious grasp, you open wider in order to understand them. In opening wider, you let a little bit more in. You stretch outward more. I must talk to two levels of you simultaneously in order for the integration to occur.

But when I am writing information into this book, I am only addressing one aspect of the reader — the conscious one.

That is not true. Perhaps you are not aware of the methods of communication that you actually use. Your writing in your books very deliberately addresses other levels of consciousness. As an example, think for a moment of Michael Tyree's artwork [in the authors' first book, *The Prism of Lyra*]. He does not consciously draw certain archetypal symbols in his art to mean something specific to the viewer. But the meaning is very clearly there without his consciously intending it. This is what happens in your writing. There are things that you convey in your writing that you will read now with your conscious mind. But you still may not consciously understand the full meaning.

I am still not getting the answer I am looking for. The best answer to my question that I can find within myself is this: You do not wish to strengthen our anchor in this reality by appearing in this reality. Therefore you will purposefully avoid this reality because you want us to go out further. We are addicted to physical reality. We will use a sighting of your craft to validate this reality and say, "This is the correct reality and we are staying here because the ship showed up and validated it for us."

That is very true. However, there is one thing we need to point out. *We are not orchestrating this.* We are not withholding your sightings in physical reality. We are allowing the natural flow of *your* own evolution to dictate what you perceive and what you do not. You, your own mass consciousness, desires evolution. It is you (the ego you) who wishes to anchor yourselves here and limit yourselves in the physical. We are complying with your wishes, but we are not imposing it upon you.

Thank you. Now let's get back to the specifics of Bobbie's dream. She said the ET in her dream could speak as male and gradually changed over to a female tone of voice.

The reason for the entity in her dream to be able to do this is very simple. This is a message that the entity itself was integrated and balanced, and can speak and touch the male and female energy. It is a complete being speaking.

What about the idea that we respond differently to male and female individuals? So the tone changed as the content of the message changed to reach different aspects of consciousness?

That is very well said, yes.

She presented an idea that people who were "aware" were marked by golden. What is that about?

Golden represents a slightly higher vibration. For instance, people who have had out-of-body experiences or astral projections have found that often when they leave their body, they observe a golden shimmer around objects that is not there when they are solidly anchored in their body. This golden shimmer is simply a byproduct of the change in dimension. When you are physical and looking through your eyes, it is a much denser reality. When you leave your body but are still in the astral, you have accelerated enough that you can also see the universal energy emanating from objects, which gives it a golden shimmer. The dream said that the communication she and others received would allow them to accelerate their vibrations enough to perceive the universal energy, or "higher level" of the world around them, which, symbolically, would shimmer golden.

116

Why aren't there more contact dreams happening?

Over the years you have received a tremendous amount of mail with very similar stories. The channel has stories of her own dreams. You have had dreams, too, but you don't remember them. These dreams are occurring *all the time.* You are simply not a society that places much importance in dreams, so very often you allow them to fade away without looking at their deeper meaning.

We will simply say that Bobbie's experience is like many others. For humans to validate only a contact that occurs in the beta waking state is to limit the entire contact experience. You are much more than your conscious minds. Your contact experiences encompass much more than your conscious minds are aware of. As you seek to understand, remember, and validate the contact you have on other levels of consciousness, you open yourself more to the integration of all the levels of your consciousness so that a new reality paradigm can be formed. The common ground will be created. It is there that we will meet each other openly. V

117

10
Integration and Transformation

"And we will all go down the labyrinth, to meet whatever awaits us there."
— Whitley Strieber
Communion

The process of integrating our consciousness has been stressed frequently by Sasha. How does this integration process transform human consciousness and allow us to prepare for contact with extraterrestrials?

In this chapter Sasha opens a door into human consciousness and encourages us to enter. Once we choose to pass through this door, we are required to explore the depths of our psyche in a way that will transform us forever.

Δ Δ Δ

Sasha: The main doorway through which many ETs choose to come to you is the door of the human consciousness. We would like to explore with you that doorway through which we enter. We would also like to explore with you what happens to you as humans when one of us comes knocking at your door. How does your reality reorganize itself so you either assimilate our contact or repress it? We will talk about that a little as well. This will give you an understanding of your inner workings and how ET contact is intricately tied to human evolution. In a sense, the extraterrestrials are part of the same dance. The extraterrestrial contact coming to your planet at this time is not only a symptom of your evolution, but is triggering that evolution.

Contact with ETs at this point in your planetary history is what is

119

supposed to happen. Any society that evolves to a certain point will eventually have to deal with a greater reality. You have put it off for quite some time. Throughout your ancient history ETs were here more openly. That has been conveniently stuffed into your memories but is just now beginning to awaken. Let us give you a peek through the door into the human consciousness.

Imagine the consciousness of an average human on your planet. The human consciousness is divided roughly into three different areas for the sake of this illustration: the conscious mind, the subconscious mind, and the unconscious mind. We would like to show you what each of these sections of your consciousness look like energetically.

The conscious mind is organized much like your computer data disks. There are blocks of information. As you are born and you go through your life, all you are exposed to becomes programmed into data blocks. Eventually, near its surface the conscious mind becomes filled with these data blocks.

So, what are the data blocks? The data blocks are all of your perceptions of reality and your belief systems. In a sense, this is the most rigid part of your consciousness. If you've been programmed with a belief system that ETs do not exist (or that you are not worthy of a visitation, or any belief), then you build a very hard wall of data blocks. These data blocks begin to form the foundation of your belief system. All of this can be accessed within the conscious mind. This affects the way you think, perceive reality, the way you live your life, and how you allow your own identity to develop. That is the conscious mind.

The subconscious mind is responsible for perceptions that are not priority. In a sense, the subconscious mind does consciousness triage. Every moment of your reality, you are bombarded with stimuli from the external and internal world such as tastes, smells, sounds, vibrations, information, etc. Some part of you has to do triage. Some part of you has to say, "This gets the attention of the conscious mind. This gets the attention of the subconscious, and this is filed away for later. This is much too scary, so let's stick it into the unconscious." The subconscious mind is the part of you that does the processing.

The subconscious mind, then, on the first level is made up of little globs of data that are awaiting processing. In your day-to-day life, if you are faced with doing something really easy and something else that is going to require a lot of struggle (or maybe it is a frightening thing), you are going to relegate the latter to the bottom of the pile. The subconscious mind will put the easiest things to deal with at the top. The scarier things get hidden under the pile. The subconscious mind is very good at procrastination.

Now let's go to the unconscious. The unconscious mind, though it is a link to your greater self, is also used as a wasteland where scary, dark things are stored that you really don't want to bring up. As information passes through the subconscious, the scariest things get put in the deepest level of the unconscious. The bottom level of the unconscious is the gateway to the higher self.

When you are a child and you have a very traumatic event happen to you (like abuse), the subconscious immediately must find a way not only to process the information and store it, but to protect you from even further fragmentation. It must then, in whatever way it can, seek to create a balance. So the very intense raw energy generated from trauma gets put deeply within the unconscious.

The unconscious is also ruled by archetypes. There is a lot that is generated in the unconscious that you are totally unaware of. Your unconscious is often triggered on a daily basis and continues to process, but it is given only a small amount of space in which to do so. (We are simplifying for this illustration.)

Now that you see the layers of your consciousness, we are going to talk to you about where ET contact fits into this. Let's say that an ET approaches you who wants to communicate. When an ET looks at you, you seem like a multiple-personality case. (We do not mean this derogatorily in any way.) This is because there are so many levels of your consciousness. The conscious mind is aware of only a small fragment of reality.

ETs often do not know how to communicate with a fragmented human. Sometimes they may fly their ships by and a few people see them. But the greater percentage do not notice, because that data gets sucked into the subconscious and the triage happens. If it is not relevant to the conscious reality paradigm, it not going to make it to the conscious mind. Therefore, you may have seen a craft, but that

121

data has not yet made its way into your conscious mind simply because there is too much data to process, and these conscious data blocks (which represent your beliefs) stop it from being remembered.

Let's say, then, that the ET tries telepathic communication. Telepathic communication comes in through the subconscious mind. Once again, the ET is faced with the same thing. He is faced with an obstacle course, depending on who you are. Some of you are getting quite adept at telepathic contact. As time goes on, your abilities to adapt to telepathic contact are increasing. The average person in society, however, does not know how to interpret telepathic contact. So once again, the telepathy given to you never makes it to the conscious mind.

You are beginning to see now that the subconscious has a well-spring of information that has been beamed at it almost since birth. Yet it is not bubbling to the surface. This is why techniques such as regressive hypnosis can start to bring out some of this information. It is starting to open doors.

Let's say, then, that the ET gets out of his or her ship while you are sitting in your backyard. The ET comes up to you and says hello. In the moment that you start perceiving us, reality starts shifting—because remember, you are one frequency and we are another. There must be a common ground between us where the contact can take place. If we are at very different ends of the spectrum, the contact becomes very difficult.

So an ET walks up to you in your backyard. Perhaps for a fragment of a moment you perceive us. But commonly what happens is that the human will suddenly shut down—usually falling into a sleep or entering a type of trance state such as one produced by alpha or theta brain waves.

If the human falls asleep (delta state), then the interaction happens on a nonphysical level. If the human enters a brain-wave reality like alpha or theta, communication may happen there. But when the human attempts to go back to his normal waking consciousness, he can't bring the memory with him. Once again, contact has happened, but you just haven't brought it through to your conscious mind.

Believe us when we tell you that every single one of you has had contact. It may have been physical, it may have been in the dreamstate, or it may have been telepathic. It may have been that you simply saw a ship. *Every one of you.* That memory is held in the subconscious.

The next questions are: How do you rearrange things in your consciousness so that contact can begin to be remembered? How can you stop compartmentalizing yourselves? First of all, the easiest place to start is with the conscious mind. Assuming you want to do this, begin examining all of these data blocks you have within the conscious mind. This means examining your conscious belief systems about your world and yourself. Some of these belief systems are not necessarily ones you consciously formed; many of them were given to you by your parents, your society, your government, or your church. That is the first step. Begin examining those data blocks and find out which ones still serve you and which ones you wish to be transformed. We guarantee that when you start doing this with honesty in looking at yourself, you are already going to start shifting.

As you do this, let's say you get rid of a couple of these data blocks. Now you have some space. Because of this space (which previously blocked the emergence of subconscious energy), some of the subconscious memories can begin coming through. Now the energy is freed up. There is not really a barrier between the levels of your consciousness. Remember, the first layer of the subconscious to begin coming through is simply the top layer of stimuli stored in the sorting process. The first layer that starts coming through is usually not scary. It represents procrastinated perceptions that are waiting for processing and recognition by the consciousness.

Let's say you start erasing more of the data blocks, freeing more energy. More and more of the upper layers of the subconscious start coming through. It will seem like a dam has burst open because so much of the energy from the subconscious is going to start shooting through.

This is what happens when someone learns to channel. In learning to channel it is essential to have a relationship with your own belief systems by understanding why you are the way you are and by seeking to always evolve the self. Then as you do that and open up, subconscious fragments start coming through before the actual clear channeling begins.

Eventually, the pathways between the conscious and subconscious mind will become clearer. Much of the data that you are getting won't be put in a corner anymore. Your processing system will become a lot more efficient. Eventually, however, you hit the bottom layer of the subconscious, which is the scariest one.

This layer is where all of your fears lie. It can be fears about death, about ETs, or any fear, however irrational it may seem. That is where they reside. They will start rising and coming to the surface of the subconscious. At this point, you have two choices. You can either seek to process them (which really cleans you out), or you can shut down and allow the emotional waves to batter you around. In that case, the repressed subconscious energy will surface in the form emotional turmoil, which you don't understand and which seems to mess up your life. It is up to you how you choose to handle this.

Extraterrestrial contact starts triggering things within the subconscious. As the data blocks free up, and as you start clearing and becoming more expansive and the ET contact starts being received, you are going to start noticing different things happening. Either you are going to begin having more ET-oriented dreams, or you are going to be thinking about ETs more, or something will have shifted that is going to be a sign (however subtle) that ET contact is indeed something real for you in your life. It's real, but it may not be tangible. That is quite all right.

Let's say all these blocks eventually get cleared out within the conscious and subconscious. The unconscious is then the last level to be dealt with. This is the archetypal level.

A positively oriented ET usually knows that for true contact to occur, you will need to be fully aligned with who you are, without repression and denial. So when ET contact starts coming in, the unconscious level becomes triggered. Think of the top layer of the unconscious as a giant pair of sunglasses. The ET "light" shines through the sunglasses and eventually makes it to your conscious mind.

ET contact will be interpreted by you through the language of the unconscious. So if your unconscious is not processed and is blocked up and houses a massive array of scary archetypes – monsters and demons – then ETs are going to be seen by you as demons. It doesn't

124

matter who the ETs are! If you've been processing many of your inner archetypes and working toward personal growth, then your consciousness will begin to shift in such a way that the light passing through the sunglasses (your interpretation of ET contact) will take on a different meaning.

Those of you who are "abductees" will find that the more you process your issues — especially your identification with being a victim — the more you turn it around and seek to learn from the experience, seeing it as a path toward evolution, and the more you actively begin taking steps to live in that way, your abductions will change. Will they stop? Probably not. Will they change? Absolutely yes. More of this is written about in [Royal Priest Research's book] *Visitors from Within*.

How you perceive ETs in your life or on your planet is a direct result of the lens through which they are seen. The lens represents your unconscious and subconscious minds. If that lens is dirty and has not been processed and healed, then your image of the ETs will be anything but pleasant.

Part of this is because we as ETs cannot enter your reality because of the vibration in which you live. Your beta reality is a tightly focused beam of energy. It takes a lot of energy to be physical in your reality. This is why you as a species need to sleep so much. In my reality, I do not have a brain-wave state that is equivalent to your beta. I cannot land my ship in a corn field, get out and shake your hand and have you remember the experience. It doesn't work because our realities don't line up.

A common ground must be created. For you to create a common ground you will need to exit (temporarily) your beta reality and enter alpha or theta. Vibrationally, those wavelengths are one of the common grounds we both may enter.

We've been meeting you on these levels since humanity began. However, the challenge is that when you have your meetings with us and then you return to the beta reality, you bump up against these data blocks and can't carry the memory of our contact through to your conscious reality. This is neither positive nor negative, but simply a part of evolution. Evolution is not just the evolution of your cells. Evolution is intricately tied to your brain and its ability to perceive multidimensionality. Your brain is the transceiver of the universal energy.

As you begin being able to tap into new frequencies on the radio dial, your evolutionary state accelerates. Once that happens, then you can get to the common ground. We then can meet, and you can go back to your consensus reality bringing with you the experience of being with us. That is where all of you are heading now.

A question you may wish to ask is, "What can I as a person do in my life right now so that I can get to the common ground?" There are some very simple things.

First, work on dissolving those data blocks. Become aware of the rigid views of reality that you hold. You may not even be conscious of these views! Begin to know who you are. Then begin to consciously change those perceptions of reality you have outgrown. Begin replacing them with new and more expansive points of view.

Next, go within, as deeply as you can. Find your own demons. Find your own fears. Find the part of you that hates yourself. Find that part of you that is not you but merely a reflection of your programming from this life and other lives. Do not abolish these things; befriend them. That is what people find very difficult.

This means looking into the mirror of your soul to see all that is there – the light, the love, and the ugliness. When you can befriend all of that, you will have gotten to the level of the unconscious. Doors will begin opening quickly. You will have begun the integrative process within your consciousness. That place is so powerful! And it is your true state of being.

You are all playing at being fragmented. This is part of your evolutionary game. It is not, however, who you are. Do not confuse your physical self (as a fragmented being) with the greater sense of your Self. Within you is a totally whole, integrated being who is sitting back watching a movie of your fragmented experiences. If you can find that Self within you, miracles will start to happen. But you have got to be willing to look at the darkness.

Many people have asked the question, "Why are the Zetas here abducting us and causing such terror?" Well, there are as many answers to that question as there are people who ask it. However, we will tell you one reason why you perceive these experiences in

126

such a terrifying manner. The Zetas represent for you a total opposite polarity — a unified whole, nonindividualistic, with no emotions. Because they represent this opposite polarity, when you interact with them you must face your own inner, opposite polarity. You must face your own darkness.

How many of you as abductees have looked into those black and shiny eyes and have seen ugliness and visions of yourself or your world that were terrifying? These are not prophecies given to you; they are simply confrontations with your own shadow. For reality itself is generated from within. The Zetas are one group of entities sent to you in your slumber, so to speak, to help awaken you into the totality of who you are. They have been called by many names. They have, to some degree (though it is accelerated now), been here throughout time. There must always be balancing forces, even in chaos. Even though everything seems chaotic right now, there is always a balance. The Zetas are helping to keep that balance.

This may not be their conscious intention. They have their own agenda. But, you are also providing for them a service that they could not get anywhere else. You represent to them their own opposite. When they look into your white and shiny eyes, they see a vision of themselves that is absolutely terrifying.

Both of you are intricately tied together in a dance of evolution. Both of you are on the brink of major realization and awakening. They are going to awaken to a greater reality and so are you. Right now, the way for you to start awakening to that greater reality is to begin clearing your blockages. These divisions within your consciousness exist only within a physical reality like yours. You are not here dealing with this because you fell from grace. You had to have been quite masterful to put yourself in such a challenging situation.

Now you have some idea what happens to you when an ET interacts with your consciousness. We hope that we have also expressed to you that you as a species are not all sitting around waiting to make contact. Contact is already happening! Some of you may be sitting around waiting for your governments to reveal it. But your governments don't have to validate your reality. *You* are the only ones who can truly say what reality is.

Start shifting and come to the understanding that contact has already happened. Each and every one of you have had it. Instead of trying to seek it, remember it. *Remember.* There is nothing to be frightened of in these memories.

One last thing. All of you recognize the great compartmentalization within your government. The left hand doesn't know what the right hand is doing. There are some segments that have ET information and some segments trying to get it. We are going to suggest to you that the state of your own individualized consciousness is a microcosm of the entire dynamic that is occurring on Earth. The way your government is compartmentalized is *exactly* the same as your consciousness.

Your government has standard propaganda that it repeats to the public. They claim that national security must be upheld. They maintain a belief that there are always enemies out to get you. Those are the data blocks through which your government sees reality.

The first few layers of the subconscious of your governmental consciousness is what is fed to the government that doesn't quite fit with their data blocks, but which they are not quite willing to discard. Some of that has to do with crashed ships. On the deeper, scarier level is the information they themselves don't want to look at. It is the stuff that will change reality itself, the information that will threaten the very integrity of the data blocks within the conscious organism. An example of this type of information might be an awareness of the abduction programs. This is such a terrifying thought to the government that it must keep this area secure. The subconscious of the governmental organism is probably the most top secret area because it holds the most fear for them.

On the unconscious level of the governmental organism is the knowledge of what is really going on. This is blocked. Trauma caused these blockages. The trauma has do with ancient extraterrestrial encounters from before recorded history.

So you see, your government as a structure is going to deal with ET contact in the same way that you as an individual will deal with it psychologically. You will either compartmentalize and keep secrets from other levels of yourself, or eventually there will be a desire to seek wholeness.

The government is not responsible for the reality of secrecy that you are experiencing. *You* are responsible for the reality of the government. As you all change individually within yourselves and open up channels through which you can integrate, the structure of the government must change because it is a reflection of you.

Your personal integration, as you prepare for ET contact and as you acknowledge its existence, is crucial. It is one of the most important things in the entire extraterrestrial phenomenon. Measuring the size of the ships and what color lights they flash is all peripheral. The most important thing is how this phenomenon changes your consciousness. As your consciousness changes, reality itself changes. If you want a different reality regarding ET contact, then you must change yourself.

You are not alone. There are thousands of us who have gone through our own evolutionary process similar to yours. We are here to hold your hand. We're not going to do it for you, but we will be there. You must be willing to take the first step, or the gap between us will not close. We will then forever stand on opposite sides of the chasm.

It is time now for that chasm to close and for us to build a bridge upon which we can meet. It all starts with you. ∇

129

11
Finding Your Truths

"We will discover truths about ourselves, truths that will change each of us — and all of us — forever. We will pierce the fog that has for so many long years obscured our vision . . . at last, we will see."
— Whitley Strieber
Transformation

The human mind records every experience that happens to us. There have even been cases where people who were in unconscious states (such as a coma, or a near-death experience) retained clear memories of things that were said or done in their room. These memories were able to be relayed verbally by these individuals after they returned to a conscious state.

But what about those memories of experiences originating from a realm outside the boundaries of the conscious mind? Can they be related verbally? Are some of our other-worldly experiences so alien to us that they remain locked within, never able to be given life through words?

In this chapter Sasha addresses how the mind and the body can be accessed in order to release some of these inaccessible memories. It seems that the key to our suppressed contact memories has been here all along. Now we simply need to unlock the door.

Δ Δ Δ

Sasha: We are going to give you some interesting information that may provide you with some exciting results. Please view this information as something that can be fun and exciting along your path to discovery; do not get caught in the seriousness of the situation. This information may provide you with some new thoughts and understandings about the contact experience. We are going to suggest several ways that you can begin knowing whether or not you've had contact and the nature of your contacts.

This may seem to contradict what we said in the last chapter when we said it is not necessary for you to go back into your past. The reason we give this information is not for you to explore your past and become obsessed there. We give this information so that when you go back into the past and find out about your contacts, you have a way to begin dissolving the boundaries between the compartments of your consciousness.

We are going to give you several techniques and suggestions that will allow you to begin hearing the language of your other compartments. You can then begin to understand the nature of the contact that you have. Some of these techniques might not have equivalents upon your world; if there are equivalents, we are not aware of them. We will attempt to simplify the technology and tell you the basic idea behind the techniques. For now we will start with some techniques that are known upon your planet.

The first is regressive hypnosis. We don't have to say much about this because most of you reading this know exactly what this is. However, we would suggest that when you go into a regressive hypnosis session you work with someone qualified. We would also suggest you work with someone in whom you have confidence. We suggest you go into the session with a specific period you want to explore, rather than going into hypnosis to try to find significant events.

Some people are easy hypnotic subjects; some are not. We would caution you here not to accept as literal fact what you receive in your hypnotic regressions. Often the information you receive is abstract symbolism which is then translated into physical reality by your conscious mind. The meaning is often not what it appears to be. Do not get caught up in the specifics; let the symbolism open you up.

Regression is one method of hypnosis that uses your verbal skills to communicate information from the other levels of consciousness. Other forms of hypnosis can convey information as well, without the use of your verbal abilities. We would suggest that this next technique, a common procedure, be used by a hypnotist who is aware of these types of procedures.

Hypnotists use the physical body to speak to the hypnotist directly. This bypasses the verbal faculties of the client, thus avoiding much censorship by the conscious mind. It looks as follows: Let's say that the hypnotist knows that during a certain week, there was a contact. When the client is in a deep state, the hypnotist can say, "If my statement is true, raise your right forefinger. If my statement is false, raise your left forefinger." In this way, the hypnotist is speaking directly to the subconscious mind. He can then proceed with statements designed to arrive at the truth. "You were contacted on Monday." The left finger is lifted (for false). "You were contacted on Tuesday." The right finger is lifted (for true). This may seem like a slow process at first, but as you establish a rhythm it can achieve astounding results. There are unlimited possibilities, and you can gain significant information about your contact experiences. The answers you receive this way do not come from your conscious mind — provided you are in fact hypnotized.

Another, similar type of subconscious questioning can happen when you are awake. You have something called "muscle testing." Basically, in muscle testing the body responds with the knowledge it holds that the conscious mind may not have. This knowledge may be which vitamin is good to take, what drug is best for an illness, or even what colors the aura likes best. You can also use muscle testing to gain information about your ET contacts. Primarily, this is beneficial for contacts that have occurred in a physical or quasi-physical state. The less physical the contacts, the less reliable muscle testing would be. If contacts occurred on an energetic or astral level, this technique loses its accuracy, though it can still be used to some degree.

We would suggest that you work with someone who is adept at muscle testing and who understands its subtleties. This person also must be able to ask you the right questions about your contact experiences. The body does not lie. Once you fine-tune your ability to let go during muscle testing, you are going to get some very interesting information from the body itself.

What would the nature of the questions be, and how do you tell a yes from a no?

That is something that the muscle tester would devise. For in-

133

stance, each person will have his own truth scale to which the body responds. Do a simple test. Say to the client, "Your middle name is Mary," then muscle test. Is the arm weak or strong? Then state, "Your middle name is Sue"(the correct answer). Is the arm weak or strong? Whatever statement is the truth would be strong, in this example. Learn the specific language for each person, and this can become quite informative.

Do you think that using this technique regularly can loosen up the subconscious? Could the compartmentalization begin disintegrating?

Absolutely. Once you get a body of information about your contacts, interesting things will begin to happen. It is very likely at the beginning that your conscious mind is going to say, "I don't believe this is true." But because the information has come to you anyway, you are going to begin thinking about it. Then a little hole in the boundaries between your levels of consciousness begins to form. It will begin letting more and more information through. If you become adept at this, pretty soon you are not even going to need the muscle testing. You will know your body's reaction before you are tested – providing you sensitize yourself.

Another tool you have on Earth is what you call the polygraph. The polygraph is not as sensitive as its creators would like to think. It does not always catch truths and untruths, but it is a start. If you want to take the time to take a polygraph test, we would suggest you write up a bunch of statements regarding your contacts that are as specific as possible. This would be a fun experiment, but not very accurate. This is a very primitive machine.

Let us take this one step further. We do not know if this exists on your world. If you can hook a polygraph machine to a living plant and then take the polygraph test, the results are going to be more accurate. Is this in use on your world?

Well, the person who invented the polygraph initially made the discovery by working with plants and he found out the plants were responding to people's thoughts and emotions.

Ah. Then this information exists within your mass consciousness, so it is a strong possibility. The plant picks up your telepathic thoughts – not just your conscious mind, but all your different levels of consciousness. The plant can "hear" your transmissions. It can relay what is truth and nontruth through the polygraph system so that you can differentiate true statements from false ones.

For another technique, we are going to ask you to think about your technology called biofeedback. This is something that can very easily be created and is similar to the polygraph. You will need to have someone professional working with you who has done biofeedback and understands the concept. He or she will teach you how to raise or lower your body temperature (or your heart rate) slightly in response to truths or untruths.

So, for instance, the first phase is a training program. The subject will be hooked to a biofeedback machine and be presented with statement after statement of untruths. The person will practice lowering his body temperature (or heart rate) slightly every time an untruth is stated. Then after he has learned to do that, he will shift to raising the body temperature (or heart rate) every time a truth is stated.

When the subject is conditioned, he or she will then be able to respond to a mixed bag of statements — true or untrue — very quickly and automatically. At that point, the introduction of statements about ET contact can then be introduced. His (or her) rapid responses can be cataloged so he can begin to see what is true and untrue.

Here is another method. We don't believe you have this on your planet (but perhaps you do in experiments in perception). It is something that could very easily be set up. Imagine a device to place over your eyes, like what your eye doctors use. Very rapidly you are going to have a flash of information given to you. Separate information will go to the left and right eyes. This information is in the form of a statement of truth or untruth regarding your ET contact. One eye will be given a statement of truth and the other eye will be given a statement of untruth. The statements are presented so rapidly to each eye that the conscious mind cannot perceive them, but the subconscious can. The tester will ask the subject which eye is receiving truth. The subject will answer quickly by either raising his left or right finger (one side will be conditioned to respond true and one to false). This procedure needs to happen rapidly so that there is no time for censorship by the conscious mind.

We have given just a few samples of processes that can be used in

135

a scientific way to test the validity of ET contact. These can also be applied to individuals who do not know if they are having contact and want information about what is going on.

We would like to reiterate that we are not giving you this information so you can take it into your laboratories and *prove* something to your logical minds. That defeats the purpose. We are giving you this information to help you begin to recognize the reality of your contacts so that the walls between the levels of your consciousness can begin to disintegrate. Then you, as an individual, naturally integrate and begin understanding the reality of the contact that has already happened.

Let this information inspire you to go forward into the realms that you've not known how to enter before. What awaits you there are many surprises and much to be learned. ∇

12
Designing Contact

*". . . with vision and perseverance, we can create a new reality, a reality
which includes the empowerment of humans to enter into a sustainable
relationship with other planetary intelligent life forms."*
— Steven M. Greer M.D.
International Director of CSETI
Close Encounters of the 5th Kind:
Contact in Southern England

Sasha has stated over and over that there is no magic button we
can press to initiate contact. However, there are things to be done
that can shift us in ways that will accelerate our *readiness* for contact.
Many of these suggestions have been explored in the previous chapters, especially in Chapter One.

Preparing for contact is a concept that we've never explored as a
sentient species ever before on Earth. We have no role models to
guide us. At some point we are going to need to stop theorizing and
take action. Soon it will be time to go out "in the field" and apply
what we've learned.

A planetary species that feels powerless and victimized may wait
for contact to be forced upon it and never take action. However,
what extraterrestrial civilization would *want* to make contact with a
powerless, frightened species? The only ETs who would want to
contact a planet filled with frightened souls would be those who want
to take advantage of them by preying on their fears. Unless we want
to create that type of contact scenario, it is time to assert ourselves
by reaching out not from fear, but simply from curiosity and excitement. The ETs have made the first step. Have we?

Some would say that projects such as SETI and Voyager are our
attempts at making contact. However, those projects were not

joyously participated in by *humanity;* instead, they were funded and implemented by governments and/or private organizations who may or may not speak for the People. Neither single individuals nor small groups (representing the People) have ever participated in those contact programs. Those projects, in a sense, speak the party line by assuming that an ET species will value science and technology (radio waves and space probes) over human consciousness. Did those contact programs speak for *you?*

Perhaps it is time to design a contact program of our own, based on our understanding of ETs, their reality, and human consciousness. With that in mind, a very inquisitive client of ours has spoken with Sasha about implementing a new contact program. That conversation is excerpted below.

Δ Δ Δ

Where would be your favorite contact location in the USA, and at what time of day?

Since I haven't actually acted out a contact, I can only tell you about my ideals. One of my first choices would be Devil's Tower, which, of course, features prominently in your movie *Close Encounters of the Third Kind.* The time windows I prefer would be sunset or 3:15 a.m. You'll find that the time around 3:15 a.m. is a common contact time because it is usually the period when the mass consciousness is quietest. That often opens windows to contact. There are other areas as well. I personally would like to make contact in the Grand Canyon area or any of the reservation areas simply because the presence of the elders on the indian reservations assists us to make an easier entrance into your reality. The elders understand multi-dimensionality more than most humans, so that would be a favorable area of contact. Those would be my two favorite spots if I were to choose.

You mentioned that ETs will act upon the human group's spontaneous readiness for contact when our conscious, subconscious, and unconscious minds momentarily align in a common vibration. You have also stated the importance of creating an exciting, expansive atmosphere surrounding the contact experience. Could you suggest an activity for the group to do at the contact site in order to bring about this alignment?

Interesting question. We can suggest something for you, though please know that this is just an example of what we mean. One example of a joint activity would be something artistic, like spontaneously creating a mural or a sculpture live in the moment. It would be as if you were given a big mural space and a bunch of paint brushes with no plan. Just begin to create the mural and have fun doing it. That is an example of being in the moment, following your excitement, and playing. This focuses your energy on something other than the contact. Often when you are focused on the contact itself, it will not occur, or it won't occur the way you expect.

If those criteria were met, hypothetically, and ETs were in the vicinity, we would key into your excitement and playful energy. If it were within our path to interact with your playful energy, we would simply find ourselves moved to be there with you to enjoy that energy. We caution you here that it may be very difficult on your world right now to get a bunch of people together to do this who do not have the silent expectation or hope or motivation to do this only because they want to make contact. They must be painting the mural, for instance, because it is what they *want* to be doing — not necessarily just to bring about contact. A contact may actually be generated when these people don't know why they are out in the desert. They may be just out there having fun, painting a mural in their excitement. That would be a prime circumstance for a contact.

It is sort of a catch-22, though. The people would be gathering for the possibility of contact. We just don't go out into the desert to paint a mural!

It *sounds* like a catch-22. The reason it does is because your reality differs so much from ours. In our reality that scenario we just described to you is very normal, not a catch-22. In your reality that type of scenario is not normal because the behavior is not normal — to go out into the desert and paint a mural. But for us, because we live only in the moment and follow our excitement, then it *is* normal behavior. The catch-22 is really only applicable here on Earth. We are simply saying the probability is higher when people are focused more on their excitement (the painting and the creative endeavor) than wishing or hoping for a contact.

The subconscious desire by humans for a contact is going to be there, and that is what we hear. But the belief that you need to sit and focus on us in order for us to find you is inaccurate. For those of you who we wish to contact, we *know* where you are. We don't need the focus of your thoughts. But often (such as in the work of some ET contact research groups conducting programs on Earth now) they *do* get response from that type of focus. Why? Recognize that the ETs are not reacting to the focused mental bodies of the research group. They are part of a greater learning process for the research group. The ETs were not called in by the processes of the group but are part of an ongoing teaching project that far surpasses the conscious awareness of the research groups. Researchers may believe that the will of the group is calling in the UFOs. No! In a sense, you could say that the ETs with whom the researchers work are the ones calling *them*, and the group is simply following the subconscious suggestions of the ETs. The research group is not the initiator of the contact, even though by human perceptions it may look that way.

What would be the ideal size for an initial contact group?

It depends upon how you envision the contact. If you are talking about a face-to-face contact, then the smaller the group, the better. If you are talking about a "light show," then the larger the group, the better, because we often draw on your energy to manifest in your reality. But these are not set in stone. It depends upon the individual circumstance.

So what numbers would be ideal for a more personal contact?

Well, we always like the number seven. Preferably not over seven. The first power number would be three, then five, then seven.

Again, this may sound like a catch-22. The more people who are there for proof and the pure nuts-and-bolts aspect of the contact, the less likely we are to show up. The more that people are there for the experience and the excitement of it, then the more likely the contact. We are not really interested in proving our existence to those who don't believe. Because of the tricks of the mind and ego, that is a never-ending cycle of problems. Some of these individuals will never believe, even if a ship lands right in front of them. Their consciousness will fragment and prevent cognition of the experience. So we prefer instead to focus our attention on people who are not there to

140

gain proof. You could have a physicist or a photographer there, as long as they were there for the enjoyment of it instead of for how much money the photos are worth.

You have said in the past that you would like a physicist, linguist, and anthropologist present at a contact site. What function would they perform?

Their function is mostly in the moment during the contact. You have no one on your world right now who could serve truly as a diplomat between ETs and humans. You would need someone who has a lot of very specialized qualities. You need someone who is psychically receptive or who has channeling abilities; you also need someone with an understanding of language structure — not because there might be a language barrier, but because when one understands language structure, one can then understand thought structure. Therefore one can learn a lot from the ETs by perceiving their thought structure. Communication can then be made more easily.

Physicists have knowledge of unseen realms and may be able to serve as a link to the group, so that the group knows that what they are seeing is not an illusion. Having an anthropologist present would put in perspective energetically the concept that if ET contact is happening here in the present, it is a given that it has happened in the past. This will open doors to the history of your civilization with ET beings so that an understanding of Earth's past can begin to be cultivated. Ideally, if you had a person on your world who was a psychic, a channel, a linguist, and an anthropologist, that person would be the perfect interface. Because you don't have one specific person who can do all this, you can divide these abilities into the different specialties and choose a person from each specialty to be there.

Would you prefer a smaller group as a stepping stone before you contact a larger group? Getting the ideal group together initially might be quite difficult.

We would prefer seven. But **the number of humanity is five**. If you had five people, it would be a wonderful statement of the recognition of your humanity. A nice touch.

Would you be willing to be at a contact site through this channel? What do you think about that?

141

People have asked us about this in the past. The only way I can answer that is in this way: If it is time for that contact, then I will be there automatically and so will the channel. However, it is not my service to promise you something when we have no intention of showing up. Do you understand? That would be a disservice.

You mean it would be a hindrance to the contact?

Yes. Unless I knew that it was the correct timing and I was going to appear, I would not want to orchestrate it with the channel.

How about the idea of Lyssa and/or Keith being there without channeling?

You would have to ask them. However, if the synchronicity were such that your group and the channel were in the same area, she might be up for it. Certainly it would be a beneficial thing, for you would have one of the preferred suggestions we mentioned — having a channel present. Again, we want to stress not to make it too structured or rigid, because that in and of itself will keep us away. That is not the way we deal with our reality.

How do you perceive the initial step taking place for making contact?

First of all, it is my understanding that before any type of major contact occurs, the mass consciousness of your planet is going to go through a shift. It is very difficult to describe what this shift entails. We have talked about the fragmentation of consciousness. There will be a shift in the mass consciousness to such a degree that the boundaries between the levels of your consciousness will lessen even more. There will then be a bleedthrough between the subconscious realm and the conscious state. If that were to happen right now as we speak, many people on your planet would be thrown into utter panic. We do not perceive it happening right away.

When this shift begins taking place in the mass consciousness, we will not land and create a major event with fanfare. Instead, you are going to notice more and more contact with small groups (one to seven or more) happening more frequently. People will be talking about it more. People will also be remembering their contacts more as well. Once this starts happening, it will be an indication that the boundaries between your levels of consciousness have begun to lessen. As these events increase in frequency, you are gradually

142

going to get acclimated to the idea of our presence, to the point where there will not need to be a big event. The small events will simply happen with more frequency, so that most of you begin having experiences and it becomes normal.

Your mass consciousness is very fragile. If we were to land with big fanfare in the middle of Dodger Stadium, the fragility of your mass consciousness might cause it to shatter. This means mass chaos on an inner level, mass panic. Much wild emotional energy would be released without control. We've seen this happen on other planets and it is not something that we wish upon your people. This is why we would rather wait for the natural tides of evolution to take you to the point where you will begin awakening to our presence and recognizing that it has been there all along than shock you awake with a mass landing.

Keep your eyes peeled. Read your literature. Listen to your radio. When you start to see more frequency of contact showing up in the media (or through word of mouth), that should indicate that the time of which we've just spoken has begun. Recognize then that the contact program has been blown wide open and you are going to see more and more contact experiences and individuals able to have them. That is how we envision the contact opening up on your world. That is what we would wish for you if we could control your contact program. But we cannot control it, because there are always loose cannons out there who may want to barge in and initiate you into the galactic community in a much more forceful way. Because of our agreements and our understandings about free will, we cannot interfere. Keep your eyes and ears open.

Could you suggest a coordinated effort toward contact based on the number five?

If someone were moved to organize grids of five throughout your planet—in sacred spots or other places—for the purpose of sending a specific vibration out to us, you might see something interesting happen. It is important for us to say that we will not respond because of the *effort* that you put out. However, if someone were to organize pockets of five people throughout your world transmitting at the same time, this human grid would cause a frequency shift on your planet, shifting the energy of your mass consciousness, then your individual energies may in turn create the right timing and draw us

143

in. This interesting project could either be very spontaneous or a coordinated effort. This could be an enjoyable experiment. It could only benefit humankind.

Could you give a closing statement to those who would like to be part of a group of five?

If you are choosing to be in a group of five, be careful of the energy you project. Possessing expectation about what should happen in these fun experiments for them to be "successful" would be a detriment. Do whatever you can to stay in the moment, to generate excitement, fun, laughter, and also open yourselves up not only to the heavens but to the Earth.

For instance, before you begin your artistic endeavor in groups of five, do a meditation. The meditation should be one to align your chakras with the colors. Start at the base of your spine, which is red. Then focus three inches below your navel with the color orange. Then focus on the solar plexus with the color yellow. Move to the heart and focus with the color green. Then move to the throat and focus on the color blue. Then move to the third eye imagining the color indigo. Then focus on the crown with the color violet. Then imagine that your crown opens and the energy from the heavens comes in through your crown, filling your entire body. Finally, imagine that your root chakra at the base of your spine opens and the energy of the earth comes through that chakra and fills your body. These two energies—the earth and the sky—meet and entwine in your heart. It is from that heart energy (which is a combination of the sky and the earth) that you express your excitement in the group of five in whatever activity you engage in.

As you participate in the creative activity, allow yourself to hold the memory of being part of a greater family—a galactic family. Let that knowledge give you a sense of security and joy. From that joy, carry on your activity without expectation. Even if no ETs make contact, you will have expressed your connectedness to your galactic family in joy, centeredness, and excitement. That can do nothing but elevate you. As you continually elevate through this exercise, you help the entire planet shift its focus and energy. This ultimately helps to shift its perceptions. This is the shift in mass conscious that we spoke about, when the contact scenario will begin to change. You will then, once and for all, begin to realize what has been here all

144

along.

Δ Δ Δ

When one takes action, the act is often more significant than the results. With this in mind, we have decided to go out in the field by designing our own contact program using some of Sasha's suggestions. The primary purpose of the following experiment is *not* to initiate contact. The purposes can best be described as the following:

1. To reach out to extraterrestrials as a symbolic gesture of desire and readiness.

2. To help dissolve the boundaries between the levels of our consciousness by challenging those very boundaries themselves.

3. To help expand the mass consciousness so that, like Magellan's natives, it can eventually begin perceiving what has been there all along.

4. To encourage a metamorphosis of the human consciousness by taking responsibility for one of the next steps in human evolution.

This research experiment will be reported in the remaining chapters of this book. Since this is written before the actual experiment, we look forward to what awaits us! ∇

13
Opening the Door to Contact

"As the world progresses towards a global civilization and an organic unity, the potential for a sustained and open relationship between humans and extraterrestrial visitors will increase. . . . It is our responsibility as humans to similarly prepare ourselves mentally, physically, and spiritually for the next step in our relationship with these visitors."
— Steven M. Greer M.D.
International Director of CSETI
Close Encounters of the 5th Kind:
Contact in Southern England

On November 20 and 21, 1993, a group of ten people were drawn together to participate in our research project. This group of ten included: Lyssa Royal, Keith Priest, Christie (massage therapist), Chris (entrepreneur & researcher), George (photographer), Kenn (computer technician), Irissa (Christie's eight-year-old daughter), Larry (printer), Louis (psychiatric nurse), and Wayne (engineer/artificial intelligence). The individuals in this group were not so much chosen as they were synchronistically drawn together.

We devised this research project using the suggestions that Sasha has made, combined with our own intuition as well as suggestions from members of our research group. We were acutely aware that even though we tried to control the planning of the project, there was another level (perhaps our own subconsciousnesses or the ETs themselves) that was assisting in the entire orchestration of the event.

Sasha had suggested in the previous chapter to break up our group into pockets of five people. Synchronistically, we had ten people, so that allowed us to form two groups of five. Before the actual event, Keith had scouted out a secluded area in the desert outside of Cave Creek, Arizona.

On the afternoon of November 20, 1993, we had agreed to drive to this secluded area and choose two separate locations (near each other) where our two groups could conduct their research. Once we arrived (and before sunset) our goal was to construct glyphs or "crop circles" using local materials such as stones and dead wood, as well as to draw glyphs in the dirt. In the previous chapter Sasha suggested that the group engage in a creative endeavor such as the creation of a mural. One of our group members (Larry) suggested that the formation of these makeshift crop circles (instead of a mural) might be an interesting message that we could send out into the universe.

When our group gathered to leave for Cave Creek, everyone was very excited. Most of the members did not know each other, so there was a natural period of time when we needed to relax and get to know one another. Before we left for Cave Creek, Sasha did a channeling for the group and some of that information is excerpted below.

Δ Δ Δ

Sasha: We know that each and every one of you have your own expectations, desires, and hopes for what is to occur within the next two days of your research project. Though we would encourage you to be aware of those expectations, we would also like to ask you to try not to let those expectations limit whatever experience you have. As you know, expectation can be one of the most potent squelchers of any type of spontaneous experience.

On my end, we have no set plan. This means that we are not putting you through an obstacle course so that you will perceive us physically. We are not going to think that if you do not perceive us you will have failed. Absolutely not! This entire experience is going to be created in the moment by what you are experiencing (both on an inner and an outer level).

Recognize that ultimately what happens on the inner level within each and every one of you is more significant in preparing you for contact than what types of ships you see or with what types of ETs you contact. On the inner level the decompartmentalization of your consciousness is essential for you to eventually begin creating the type of contact experiences that you would like to have. So, more than anything else, this experience will be an exercise for you and

148

your inner world – how you can begin evolving to a point where experiences outside of normal reality will no longer be kept from your conscious mind.

All of you who are here in this group have had experiences of an ET nature that you do not remember consciously. If we were to say there is one goal for us, it would be to help you to become more in touch with your methods of decompartmentalization so you can begin integrating yourselves and creating the perfect stage upon which contact can begin occurring.

There are going to be many energies around you. Simply know that you are part of an experience that is meant to be fun. Secondly, this experience is meant to teach you something about yourself and your own perceptual abilities. If anything else happens beyond that, it is a plus for you. This is more for you to experience some inner aerobics so you can begin having the contact that you would like.

Before we continue, are there comments or questions on what we've said?

I have something I would like clarified. You and your group and our group are not the only ones involved. Let's say as an example that we have our group here. Let's say that some of our friends heard about what we are doing and were excited to have their own gathering at the same time we are doing ours. Well, there are other ETs out there aware of our experiment and they will, in a sense, have their own gatherings to interface with our experience.

Yes. From our end, we are seeing this as a research project also. Each ET group will hook into the energy of it to learn what they want to learn as well.

Some of you have noted the number of males and females in your group. There is a greater percentage of males. Besides Lyssa, the other adult female (Christie) is also one of the token channels, as we have suggested previously. You could consider her "staff," so to speak. This leaves, then, a girl child and a group of men. Interesting balance, yes?

The reason for this is because your group is meant to be symbolic of the mass consciousness. You are, in a sense, a microcosm of the mass consciousness. Within your mass consciousness, the dominant energy is male, or masculine energy. As representatives of the mass

149

consciousness, the changes that occur within all of you are going to be helping the mass consciousness as well. It was very important that whoever was drawn to this experience be a reflection of the mass consciousness. How perfect!

The female child is representative of the growing feminine energy that is still, as a child, within the mass consciousness. She represents the playfulness and childlike energy that is awakening within a masculine-dominated mass consciousness.

Let us explain to you about the glyphs (or "crop circles") that you are going to create. [The term "crop circle" is often used to denote the glyphs that the group made.] Each person will be responsible for one segment of the crop circle. Think in your mind of what a crop circle looks like. Sometimes there are many circles connected by different pathways.

If there are five people in your group, the first person will be responsible for a circular pattern. The second person will be responsible for a connecting point. The third person will be responsible for a circular pattern and the fourth person will be for a connecting point. The fifth person will be responsible for the final circle. In this way, you will all be working together but still expressing your own individual creativity. You'll be connecting the glyphs together to form a complete creative endeavor.

So, what time is the landing, Pleiadian Standard Time? (laughter)

You may lock him in the trunk tonight, if you wish!

When I was reading the first draft of the book, I got to the part where your colleague had an encounter with a human named Janice. You said she became very sleepy. As I was reading this, I became very sleepy and dozed off. All of a sudden I was in a room that was unfamiliar to me and was handed this enormous crystal. I was being shown things inside this crystal and then was instructed to hold it up to my head. I did so and don't remember anything after that. Then I woke up and continued reading the book.

Wonderful! A perfect example of decompartmentalization. You were reading about the contact experience and about the human woman becoming sleepy. You then experienced the same phenomenon and went right into a contact experience of your own.

150

You then woke up and returned to your reading while maintaining a sense of continuity. Perfect!

The crystal was symbolic of your crystallized memories that you are awakening. Holding it up to your head was a way of activating your memory. Also, when you held it up to your head you helped to open up the various levels of your consciousness. Very interesting dream.

After reading the manuscript I dreamt of a brown fluffy dog that I was helping to bring to the common ground!

You were exercising your understanding and abilities of getting to the common ground. You not only were practicing bringing yourself to the common ground, but also helping to bring your mass consciousness there as well.

In that dream there were also Mexicans, but even though I don't speak Spanish, I could understand them.

Those Mexicans represent the idea of "alien." You could understand their language, though! That is an indication that you did enter the common ground with them.

Also in the dream there were these round disks. I was helping Pleiadian people move these disks (which were underground).

This is symbolic. The memories of contact throughout history are buried very deeply within the landscape of your mass consciousness. You were helping to dig them up!

We are very excited about all these dreams you've had as you were preparing for this excursion. This is telling you that something else is happening on a deeper level.

It is important that during your experience, you achieve a group energy. We often find it very difficult to contact your planet because your mass consciousness is so fragmented. You do not see yourselves as a People. It is very important that you all see yourselves as a group. Even though you may break up into two groups of five, think of yourselves as still linked together.

We will depart for now. Have a good time!

151

Δ Δ Δ

It was about 4:00 p.m. when we arrived at a remote location outside of Cave Creek. We drove on an off-road path with snow-capped mountains surrounding us until we came to a hill to which we were intuitively drawn. Breaking up into two groups of five, we each chose our area in which we would construct our glyphs. We had a short period of time until sunset, so we set about completing our task.

Each group began to construct its glyphs. Generally, they took the form of traditional crop circles with a mixture of circular glyphs and connecting bridges in between. Each group found that they became very playful and focused on the task — hardly even looking up into the sky at what might appear. Some participants became very creative and incorporated Native American Anasazi-type glyphs within their circle. Irissa, Christie's eight-year-old daughter, constructed an elaborate Zeta Reticuli face with huge eyes filled in by quartz and amethyst crystal.

When we had finished our task, we set about collecting firewood before it became too dark. Soon both groups had roaring fires and all of us met on a hill between our two circles. There, Sasha conducted a brief meditation designed to bring in the Earth energy, the star energy, and integrate it within the heart of the person. After the meditation, we returned to our group and began to settle ourselves close to the flames. One by one, we spoke openly to the group about our personal contact experiences. The types of experiences people recalled varied from no memory of any experiences, to having seen ships at close range and everything in between. Some of the participants were aware of "abduction" memories but hadn't explored them fully.

As we spoke, the energy changed. We all began to open ourselves to each other and felt a strong sense of camaraderie. At times we would focus on moving lights in the sky, only to realize they were airplanes. It became clear, however, that the focus of this event was not outside of ourselves. In opening to each other, in a sense we opened to ourselves. Some of the participants later reported feeling "euphoric" and enjoyed the evening most profoundly.

At one point about two hours into our experience, the groups joined around one fire. There we sat with a panoply of stars above us, a roaring fire, and in the company of people with like minds. As the group sat warm and contented around the fire, Lyssa began to channel Bashar, which was a surprise to us all.

Δ Δ Δ

Bashar: Allow us to say greetings this night to each and every one of you. Are you having a good time? So are we. We all enjoy the parties that you create for yourself and the doorways that you open through which you wish to travel.

We are here this night as a representative for you of the group that you call "Association." As you (as a species, as a planet, and as a people) prepare for contact, you automatically, in a sense, fill out your application for membership. Do not take us too literally. You are in that sense already members. However, you simply have not yet recognized it as a whole.

So this night we reach out to you as equals and partners. We say congratulations that you as a representative of your mass consciousness have taken the steps (however small they may be or feel) toward a unification, a confrontation, a sharing. Congratulations for the energy that all of you have chosen to participate within by being here this night.

This is much more than contact in the traditional sense of the word. As some of you already have stated, you are contacting yourself. You are, in a sense, confronting another portion of yourself that you have allowed to hide and be fragmented. In contacting that portion of yourself you open doors to the universe that are much more significant than you consciously realize at this time. Recognize that your group, like other groups who are now initiating contact, is doing it because you have evolved your consciousness to such a point where you realize it can be done. You now realize you have had the ball in your hand the entire time. Recognize that for you to be doing this, your mass consciousness is shifting, for you and your mass consciousness are one and the same. You are a microcosm. Whatever you do is reflected in the whole.

153

Do not underestimate the significance of your gathering — whether or not any of you have any physical sightings or experiences. This is much less significant than the actual bonding you have done and the energy you have put out. That energy you have put out is like extending your hands to us. Though some of you may be joking about the artistic value of your crop circles, [laughter] recognize that we are not laughing at you.

Your crop circles in themselves were your own interpretation. What you all created individually in your own segment of the crop circle and as a whole were very representative of who you are, what you desire, and how you see the universe. So, as you have previously suggested, they are like cosmic Rorschach tests. They are quite impressive.

You embodied, within your crop circle design, some of the fundamental archetypal energy that is being released within the human consciousness. This is also what is embodied in the crop circles that you find upon your world. The vibrations that you have created in your group crop circles is very, very similar to the vibration when one of us performs a crop circle for you. It is the same intent. For we all come together, we have fun, we become artistic, in a sense, and we simply allow the natural energy to translate itself into your reality as it naturally would. Even though it seems as if you were planning what you did, still in the moment you allowed it to channel through you. What you set out to do was powerful indeed.

Even though you may or may not be aware of it, you performed a ritual. Each of you had a role and you went about performing this ritual and connecting your ritual steps together into a cohesive whole. Then each group met at a common ground (a center point) and performed a meditation. There all the energy you had generated in your crop circles came together and tied into you as a group.

As Sasha has spoken about, the value of some of the Native American rituals is profound in unlocking your consciousness and decompartmentalizing you. You, tonight through your ritual, took another step toward decompartmentalization. So you may give yourselves a grand pat on the back.

Has what we've said made sense to you? Are you getting the feeling of the success of your experience? Do not sell yourselves

154

short in that way. Know that the inner experimentation that you do tomorrow is not so much to release memories of experiences you have had tonight, but primarily this regressive work will be another way to help decompartmentalize. It will help you to crumble the walls between the layers of your consciousness. This entire weekend is devoted to melting those layers and integrating yourselves. It will allow you to move (however slowly it may seem to you) to that common ground where suddenly one day you will realize you have been all along. Because the terrain of this common ground is so alien (no pun intended), you have not recognized it. Each of you has been there and knows what it looks like. Now you will learn to sustain it and make it part of your greater reality. How exciting!

I told some of my friends about this experiment and it felt important that I did, as if they were participating in the energetic aspect of it.

Absolutely so. For this energy of what you have created must spiral outward into your mass consciousness. If you contain it, you will not spread it. What you have done must also reach the conscious mind. Just spreading the energy of this experience on the mass conscious level is not enough. It must also spread on the conscious level so that the disintegration of the walls can occur. And so the publication of this information will help to achieve that, as well as your discussing this experience with your friends.

When we do the exploratory work tomorrow, what areas do you suggest we focus upon?

For those of you performing the regressions, take the person to one past experience. Explore one past experience that may have been compartmentalized within the consciousness. Then also ask those persons while in the hypnotic state to pick a specific time frame during this experience tonight. Their mind will automatically move to a particular experience to which they are drawn. Have them explore that experience from the higher-consciousness point of view. We would leave this open to you and your own intuition, but we would suggest you regress them back to sleep state of this night tonight. Search for any dream encounters that may happen. Take them back and let them do their exploration. Most of all, follow your guidance as to where to take them and/or they will know where to go intuitively.

So there are three specific areas to explore. One would be contact that has happened in this life expression for each individual. The second one would be a point during this experience tonight. And the third would be what occurs in the dreamstate.

That is correct. Have a good time.

I was up at Bandelier National Monument [outside of Santa Fe, New Mexico] with my friend recently, hoping to make contact of some kind. There we "accidentally" met you [through Bashar's primary channel, Darryl Anka]! Now I am here, and here you are again. Why was I there and why am I here now?

Very simply, you are preparing for contact. Your consciousness will lead you to the experiences you need to have in order to dissolve those boundaries within your consciousness.

One of the things you had wanted to create was a *physical* encounter or contact that would allow your conscious mind to begin solidifying the reality of extraterrestrials. What better way than to create contact with an extraterrestrial you already know? So in that sense, though I am not able to be there physically on your world at this time, I am able to be there through my channel [Darryl Anka]. You synchronistically created contact with one of the ETs whom you know best. How very creative of you!

In terms of physical contact, is the Association looking for ambassadors for that event?

The Association considers each and every one of you ambassadors. There is in that sense no hierarchy or choosing. You choose yourselves. Any of you who chooses to be an ambassador may be one.

Is physical contact something that you are interested in? It seems like you are more interested in dreamstate, past-life, and future-life contact.

It is not so much that we are holding ourselves back from physical contact. It is simply that we engage in contact in the only way *possible* at this time. The only way possible in the greater sense at this time is through the dreamstate or other-reality states. Those are the most common and easiest places for us to meet you. In terms of physical contact now, the realities do not align, so we allow contact to occur in whatever way possible.

Always interpret your dreams, first and foremost, on the symbolic level for what they mean to you and your mass consciousness. Above and beyond that, we leave it up to you to apply them to your physical lives. If all of you could actually remember everything you dream every night you would be astounded to see exactly how much preparation for contact you have achieved. For now, you remember consciously what is needed to be remembered in order to assimilate it gradually into the mass consciousness. If a good portion of you remembered much more at this time, then in a sense, it would overload the mass consciousness. You, as extensions of the mass consciousness, are simply serving in the best possible way for the mass consciousness. It is not so much personally related to you as it is related to you as part of the mass consciousness.

When you rest, do you dream? If so, do you remember your dreams?

My life is one waking dream. What you experience as dream reality is to us normal, waking reality. We have dream images that flit in and out of our reality, but it does not cause dissociation for us as it does for you. You will eventually get to a point where your dream realities will begin blending with your daily realities. We know this is beginning to happen already for many of you. Therefore, eventually you will create the same type of reality that we have. Though I do at times engage in meditation, the experiences are much more experiential than they are intellectual. So to me, an internal experience is equal to an external experience. It is the same one thing.

Do you have any suggestions for us to remember our dreams?

We have many suggestions. It will depend upon your own preferences. Program one of your alarm clocks to go on with soft music at approximately 3:15 a.m. Allow yourself to gradually be roused from slumber. Train yourself to bring forth from the depths of the subconscious the experience that you were having at that time. If it is something you wish your conscious mind to remember, then have a tape recorder or pen and paper next to the bed to record it. This is one suggestion. Another suggestion is to learn some of the techniques that are spoken about in a book on your world called *Lucid Dreaming*.

Do you ever experience something that you don't quite understand?

My reality is such that understanding with the intellect is not necessary. You on your world are concerned with understanding intellectually and understanding emotionally. You make separations between those two within you. Therefore, you find that understanding often eludes you because of that rigid focus and that compulsion. In our reality we are integrated to the point where there is an understanding that occurs, but it is an understanding like the term you call "grok." [This is a term introduced in Robert Heinlein's book, *Stranger in a Strange Land*.] This is not an intellectual understanding, but instead a knowingness on all levels of the being. In that sense, no, there is nothing that ever confounds us. However, we understand that if we do not "grok" it in its totality, at some point we will. We too like surprises.

We would at this time like to express to you our gratitude for your pioneering, for your breaking ground upon which to lay the foundation for the common ground that will be created. It is our privilege, our joy to work with you in this way, and be part of the unfolding of something that has been long awaited by many of us — your sovereignty and self-recognition as a planetary species. It is then that you will be able to step into our open arms. As that day approaches, we look forward to it. We encourage you further, and we ask that you do not doubt yourselves and do not ever stop moving forward. Have patience. Trust in yourselves and your planet and all those who guide you. We will be with you in your dreams to help you to learn how to bring your dreams into the reality that you know.

Much love to each and every one of you. We bid you happy dreams.

Δ Δ Δ

The fire began to die down and it seemed natural to close our gathering after the channeling had ended. Together we put out the fire and gathered our crop circle materials that we had brought with us. Once the cars were loaded, we all sat in our vehicles quietly for a final five-minute silent meditation.

Though our group did not experience any dazzling UFO sightings or physical encounters with ETs, something certainly shifted within us. This became more apparent as we conducted our regressive research on Day 2, and in the following days after our adventure. ∇

14

Pieces of the Puzzle

"In the world of extraordinary encounters, seeing is destiny."
—Kenneth Ring Ph.D.
The Omega Project

"Do you remember ever seeing any UFOs, Irissa?"

"No. I've only seen a spaceship."

That is the perspective of the UFO/ET phenomenon through the eyes of an eight-year-old child. To her, the experiences she has had are not of an unknown origin. Instead, they are part of a greater reality that we as adults have learned to filter out of our daily lives.

After the airing of the TV movie *Intruders* in 1992, Irissa explained to her mother that the Visitors she has seen are not quite the same as the ones depicted in the film. She went on to describe, in detail, the shape of their feet. This description was not fraught with fear and terror, but an objective recalling of the details she had remembered. Irissa has gone on to educate some of the young children at her school. She and her friends draw spaceships and speak to each other of their encounters. Perhaps Irissa and her friends will grow up to become some of the first extraterrestrial anthropologist research teams!

A key to the transformation of the ET contact experience has to do with how we perceive the experience — on both the conscious and subconscious level. At this point in time, there is still a gap between the two. Perhaps we need to become more childlike in our willingness to discover the unknown.

In order for us to shift our perceptions, we must make a conscious effort to discover how we actually limit an expansion of our reality by the thoughts we project. We also limit ourselves by the language

159

we use ("UFO" rather than spacecraft), our habitual exclamations ("I don't believe it!") and our ready dismissal of unidentified lights as airplanes or weather balloons. Without a conscious effort to *make room* in our reality for a paradigm shift, there will be no place to house our new perceptions.

This is why regressive hypnosis has been so valuable on such a mass level. As it unlocks repressed memory, it frees up the human consciousness to assimilate new ideas and incorporate them into the whole consciousness. In this way, shifts of perception can be born. It is for this reason that we conducted regressive hypnosis sessions with the research group who participated in the creation of our crop circle glyphs.

In this chapter we are going to present excerpts from some of our sessions of regressive hypnosis. These excerpts are not meant to "prove" that contact happened for our group, but rather to allow you, the reader, to get a feel for the inner shifts in perception as well as the catharsis that the person experienced.

It is very difficult to separate the ET contact phenomenon from the theme of spiritual transformation. This theme made itself known in each regression that we conducted. Each subject experienced a profound spiritual connection with the nonterrestrial being who made contact. We suspect this happens for each and every person contacted; however, only some individuals are aware of it consciously. Still others choose to process the negative and fearful aspects of the experience before a shift in their consciousness is made.

During these regressions, we focused on two main areas. In the first section, we asked the individual to recall their experiences in the desert on the previous evening. In the second section, each person was asked to recall his or her dreams on the evening of our contact research project. We did not print the regressions of each group member here for various reasons. Some could not be deciphered on tape and therefore could not be used. Other subjects simply recalled mundane events. For the sake of brevity, we give you the highlights below.

The first regression we will relate is that of Chris. In his regression, he recounts a familiar theme — that of making contact with one's own reincarnational future self. Below, he recalls under hypnosis what he perceived during our experience in the desert:

Chris: "Bashar was watching us . . . from way above. Watching as we made the crop circles and that all of our future selves might have been there as well, looking down at us. Playing. And we have to meet them halfway. I perceive a large triangular spacecraft high above our atmosphere but also very close. Observing us. Waiting to meet their past selves when their past selves are ready to . . . unite with the future selves."

Is some part of you seeing this craft, or is the perception of a different nature?

"I'm not seeing the craft, but at this moment I am remembering it. A minute ago I was seeing it. Large triangular craft with many beings aboard . . . looking down. My future self was on board and was on board [when I was] at Bandelier [National Monument outside of Santa Fe]."

Are you aware of the presence of any other beings?

"I think there were some Pleiadians. They were together. Members of the Association . . . Sasha . . . "

What about her?

"She was with them."

She was not on her craft?

"No."

What other races were represented?

"I don't know. Essassani, Pleiadian . . . can't see . . . I think in my dreams last night I talked about the regression today with Bashar or somebody."

When you were with the group and were aware of Bashar and the Association, what feeling comes to you about that? What implication for you?

"That I have a future self I will meet someday. But I'm not ready yet. Right now the foundation is just being laid for that event."

What do you need to do to make that foundation firmer?

"Meditation. Raise my vibratory frequency. Healthier living."

In speaking with Chris after his regression, he seemed profoundly moved by his experience. Whether there was actually a ship present or not, this inner experience provided a strong transformational energy within his consciousness. Whether real or imagined, he was changed.

George experienced a similar catharsis during his regression back to the evening of our research project.

George: "... I see ships."

Can you describe those ships?

"I'm reminded of a dream I had when the ships were in the sky. I seem to see them along the horizon, above the horizon."

Which direction?

"Toward where Lyssa was [to the north] ..."

What happens once you sight them?

"What comes to mind is slow motion . . . I see myself walking around picking up the wood."

What significance did these ships have for you?

"It would be a confirmation of what I was doing . . . of the whole process."

And did you get that confirmation?

"Yes. I felt the confirmation even without the hypnosis . . . I just feel very comfortable seeing saucers in the sky. It's a very comfortable feeling to see that."

Was there anything else that occurred that you need to experience here?

"What comes to mind is a good energy that is going through my body."

And where is this energy emanating from?

"I guess it's coming from the sky . . . It is a connecting energy."

Between what?

"It is a connecting energy between me and everything that is."

Once again, the regression revealed a positive experience that provided spiritual insight. Later, George spoke of feeling relieved after the regression, as if an energy that was once repressed was

162

released.

Under hypnosis, Wayne did not recall anything other than what he perceived consciously. But he did have some interesting thoughts on the subject of our personal contacts:

Wayne: "I saw a red streak to the western sky, very red . . . the significance is that when that type of event happens I realize at that moment that we are not alone. They are around us or with us.

"One of the things that has me into this type of field in the first place is the idea that there is some kind of secret life, another part of you that is making arrangements, doing things that affect the conscious part of you."

Wayne's comments seem right on target. They describe the flavor of Kenn's experience, recounted below, that was recalled under hypnosis. Kenn begins his session speaking as himself. But as his hypnosis deepens, he begins speaking as the extraterrestrial being who contacted him — perhaps revealing the "secret life" to which Wayne referred above.

Kenn, what are you seeing?

Kenn: "My future self, apparently . . . . It's impossible. But at the same time, it is me. If that's so, why have I chosen to be here on this planet?"

What do you look like?

"Zeta Reticulum. Yet I chose to be here, also."

What is this being's mission?

"Exploring deep, deep space, infinitely far away. Apparently, new reaches. It's beautiful . . . . That's our mission . . . to watch. We're over a continent surrounded by water on three sides . . . watching . . apparently North and South America. I get [the year] 2085, but that seems mighty strange."

What is this entity aware of in relation to that area?

"The water is blue instead of green."

Why is that?

"Not enough algae."

How did that come about?

"They don't listen . . . they continue to pollute."

Who is "they"?

"The people of Earth."

Are you in open contact with the people of Earth at this time?

"Of course."

When did that come about?

"2061."

How was it received?

"Violently."

Explain.

"The majority of their governments think that any outside contact is a threat as opposed to an assistance. And although they had contact with us for a long time, they only want it for weaponry."

Are there other races in contact with the Earth humans at this time? Prior to 2061, overtly?

"Yes, overtly."

When was the first public, overt contact between the Earth human governments and nonTerran species?

"Early '50s."

When did the governments acknowledge this as fact and allow the open viewing of ET individuals to the public?

"2072."

You raised a question before about why you, the human, are allowed to see this future self. Why? Why, if this is your future self, did you become an Earth human?

"To get a clear view of what it's about and how they act and interact with each other and outside forces or energies."

Does this future self remember its past life as a human?

"Oh, yes. Very instrumental in achieving greater understanding. But still very hard to understand why . . . this species chooses to push things to the brink in every situation before they act in a proper manner. Too much ego."

What suggestions would this future self have for you now? What

164

would it ask you to do now or explore?

"To wake up to who we are. Stop being in fear of any changes or anything. Start doing the things that are constructive in life. Start being the energy source he is [in order] to allow the knowledge of past, present, and future to work with and through him. To bring a quicker and [more] complete understanding to those around him who can and will listen."

Have you as an Earth human in this life expression met him? Have you had contact with him?

"My initial response is, of course."

When was the first occasion?

"I get a year, but no memory of it. 1973. And last night."

Speak of last night's contact. When did it take place last night?

"When we were standing and sitting around the fire down in the lower area. I walked off into the crop circle we had created. There were two of us there with him. Although he didn't see us, he felt us."

What occurred during that contact?

"It was a reunion. He will wake up soon to his potential, which, like the rest of you, is great."

Before we return him to his normal waking consciousness, is there anything further that needs to be said?

"That we care for him and you all. And you've made a wonderful start here. We ask you to continue."

As one can imagine, Kenn was stunned after the completion of this session. He too felt a profound shift in his consciousness that lasted days after our group was together.

This entity mentioned that in his time line, contact was received by Earth's people "violently" and that the governments were the opposing force to their presence. It is important to remember that this represents only a *possible* future, and we still have the power to change the course of our planet's contact scenario. We can do this by no longer allowing our governments to dictate the pace of our first-contact program. If we take our contact program into our own hands as a People, it is then that the governments will follow.

165

DREAM EXPLORATIONS

Since many contacts seem to occur during sleep, we chose to explore the dream states of our research group on the evening of our project. Once again, the information revealed through hypnosis about the prior night's dream experiences was profound indeed. We will begin with Chris:

Chris: "I had many dreams about yesterday's events, but they are blocked. All of my other dreams are easy to remember, but the ones regarding what we were doing up there yesterday I . . . I know I was talking to Bashar about today, about this regression. It's confusing."

Is there some part of you that has an objection toward remembering these dreams?

"(Surprised) I think there might be."

Chris's experience of blocked memory is not a unique one. There are countless stories related through regressive hypnosis of a contact memory deliberately being blocked. It brings to mind Wayne's earlier statement of our "secret life" — a part of us that makes arrangements that affect the conscious aspect of ourselves.

George, however, had vivid recall under hypnosis of his dream experience the night of our research project:

George: "The first thing I see is a guy sitting at a computer. He seems like a pretty regular guy. He's a male. It's a flash in my mind."

What was he working on with the computer?

"The word that comes to mind is 'balance.' He is balancing things. Balancing energy."

Who is this person?

"I don't know. He is a friend. He is playing that computer like a piano."

Does he have any message for you?

"I guess I see myself at the computer now."

What is coming up on the screen?

"I see different members of the group on the computer screen — Lyssa, Larry . . . Chris, Wayne . . . they seem to roll up the computer screen. I'm looking at it kind of in awe. There's some kind of

166

connection. It's almost like I'm being shown how things are working. I feel really excited, like I want to do it. I want to do it . . . I want to run the computer."

Is there anything else from your dreamstate that you'd like to review?

"Well, I just saw myself flying in the air. I see myself connected with wires . . . connected to different kinds of energy, different colors pulsating. I see yellows, oranges, and reds. There are a lot of blinking bright lights – at the computer, at these tubes going into my body. They are really pretty, almost like neon in Las Vegas. The energy is real good."

So what is the significance of this for you?

"A nice dream! Really positive. I think it's an energy that enables me to go past my limitations now, my mental barriers about what is possible and what is not. Very old barriers I've set up for myself that I'm ready to go through now. It feels very timely. I feel like I'm in touch with my strength as opposed to being in touch with the regular stuff. The tubes always had the negative stuff in them."

Once again, the subject experienced a profound spiritual upliftment after searching for contact experiences within the catalog of repressed memory. Though this dream can be interpreted literally as a contact experience or symbolically as transformative energy within the psyche, probing the hidden layers of the mind has once again triggered a sense of healing and completion.

We will explore one more dream memory revealed under hypnosis that produced a profound affect on the dreamer – Wayne.

Wayne begins by insisting, while under hypnosis, that he cannot remember his dreams. But as he is taken deeper into the hypnotic state, he begins to recall seeing the "face" on Mars. He goes on to recall climbing around the terrain of Mars with a female in a jumpsuit:

Wayne: "From a distance she looks humanlike, but up close she looks more insectlike. Six limbs. Small head, but a big head compared to the thin neck. Heart-shaped head. Eyes very compassionate. A sense of maternalistic, very motherlike. Kind of stroking, stroking my back. It is almost like this is on an ant hill . . ."

Is there communication between you and this insectlike individual?

167

"There is communication in the sense that I am picking up feeling. As far as words . . . She kept calling me 'my son,' and saying, 'It is so good to see you. It's been a long time.'"

Talk about the feelings.

"I don't have this bonding feeling that she seems to have. It's been too long. I don't know what our relationship really is. I'm comfortable, but I don't feel that is where I really belong. There is one message from her: 'For most, being human is a way to experience. For you, being human is a way to leave experience.'"

After all the regressions were completed, our group met to discuss our perceptions. For those people who had hypnotic recall, there was no question that the experience was a transformative one. The recalled memories helped them to put their contacts in perspective and opened whole new doors through which they can now explore. We suspect that the hypnotic probing will also rearrange blockages in the psyche leading to more avenues through which they can explore and eventually assist in the integration of their consciousness.

While the regressions were continuing in other rooms and before we discussed the results of some of the regressions, we decided to conduct more experiments. As Sasha suggested, we tried some alternative methods for receiving information about contact. Though we would not rely on these results as a sole source of information, we report our discoveries below.

George brought along his pendulum, which assisted us in choosing the Cave Creek area. While one of our group was still in regression, several of us sat around and posed questions to the pendulum. The pendulum can only answer a yes or no question, but can also denote the strength of the answer. These are the results:

1. Was there a craft present at the crop circle site last night? *Yes.*

2. Did it land? *Yes.*

3. Did we have physical contact last night? *Yes.*

4. With more than one group? *Yes.*

5. Were they working together? *No.*

6. Will we be ready for physical contact as a group and consciously remember it within a year? *Strong yes.*

7. Within six months? *Strong yes.*

8. Within three months? *No.*

9. Did the occupants of the craft that landed come out? *No.*

10. Did the craft make any sound? *Yes.*

11. Was the ship that landed Pleiadian? *Yes.*

12. Was Sasha on that ship? *Strong yes.*

13. Was Bashar on that ship? *Strong no.*

14. Was there a possibility that they would have shown themselves to us? *No.*

15. Was there any landing evidence left out there? *No.*

What is interesting about this pendulum session is that as Kenn was still in regression, he obviously had no knowledge of the results of the test. When he emerged from the session (having gained some repressed memory of last night's experience), he confirmed several key points that were revealed by the pendulum. This was a nice little validation that simply added more excitement to the entire weekend's experience.

Δ Δ Δ

At the close of our research weekend, we assembled in the backyard for some final comments from Sasha. She also gave the group an opportunity to discuss their experiences while being regressed.

Sasha: Greetings. We would like to speak to you about an overall sense of what you experienced. This entire experience, first and foremost, was for you as individuals. Within your own individual experience, there is meaning for you. There is very much to learn about yourself by looking at what you did or did not experience. We will leave it up to you to find significance in your own experiences.

To repeat what was said yesterday, each of you represents a portion of the mass consciousness. What you did or did not experience, and the emotions that you felt because of it, is also a miniature version of what the mass consciousness will feel during any type of mass contact program.

Each of you fulfilled a role. Each of you had a unique experience.

169

We would have been very surprised if your experiences were all the same, because contact in and of itself is unique for each individual. It is always a reflection of who you are within. The fact that each of you had different experiences but yet at the same time there was an overlapping flavor, is very accurate regarding what is really happening on a deeper level. Each of you, being individuals, will automatically generate an individual experience. But as a whole (in looking at it from the bird's-eye view) you all overlap. All together you create a complete tapestry.

From our point of view as we watched your experience last night, you set out to create the environment that you wanted to create. We watched your energy fields while you were doing the crop circles. What was very exciting to watch is that as you were doing the circles, for the most part you were very focused. You were having a good time. You were activating the childlike energy within you, which is so very important to help you begin laying a foundation to prepare for contact. Without that foundation, the true experience of contact cannot be created. We are very different from you. Our reality is very childlike. Therefore, you must go within to find your child, and that is also one of the areas of the common ground between us — that childlike energy.

Another thing that you did during your crop circle experience was begin communication on a level that is nonverbal. This nonverbal level is also the beginning of the creation of a common ground. Obviously, we do not speak your language. Even if we knew English, it is not our native language and our own perceptions are not reflected through that language. You do not speak our language. So there must be a center point somewhere upon which we may communicate. The whole idea of symbolic communication, whether through glyphs or pictograms, means something very deep within the consciousness on a level that we can both meet upon.

There is something else that we want to address. This is very, very significant. We wanted to tell you this *after* you had the experience.

When intelligent entities wish to begin making contact, it means they recognize themselves and the other beings as sentient. When they wish to bridge a gulf, there is one behavior that is a signpost of sentience. That behavior is mimicry. Chimpanzees mimic humans. It is their attempt at bridging a gulf. In communication with dolphins, there is mimicry. Also, when humans set out to make contact with gorillas in the forest, often the humans mimic gorilla behavior. This is a very important first step in reaching out to another species. What you did by making your crop circles is mimic the behavior of the ETs. Not that your group is the only one to think of this, but those of you around the world who have thought of this and have begun doing it are sending out one of the most powerful messages yet sent to the ETs. By your mimicry, you are first of all recognizing your own sentience. Second, you are recognizing the sentience of those visiting you. And finally, you are attempting to meet in the middle by speaking the only conscious language you know of that those you are trying to contact can understand.

This experience of mimicry on your part is the *first* strong indication that you as a species are awakening to your sentience and beginning to reach out and contact other species. Do not underestimate the power of this. The more that you all do this upon Earth—whether it be mimicking crop circles, making model UFOs and flying them, or any other behavior that you perceive UFOs and ETs do, you are going to be opening a doorway that was previously closed.

When the ETs begin to see that you are mimicking them, they will give you more complex things to mimic. You will then begin mimicking those more complex things. A common language will be built. Another common ground will be formed. The whole process of opening to contact will be much more rapid indeed.

This is a milestone in human history, at least from our point of view. It says to us that you are getting out of bed and rubbing the sleep out of your eyes, and beginning to see not only yourselves, but another reality with which you wish to interact. Congratulations.

Keith, do you have further comments on this?

Yes. There is a principle that we can apply to any of this. When we are dealing with the ETs, we are dealing with ourselves. If we are mimicking the ETs, we are in a sense mimicking ourselves or an internal part of us. The glyphs are an attempt at communicating with the other compartmentalized aspects of ourselves as well as with the ETs. I'm not saying, however, that the ETs are totally our creation without a reality of their own.

Our suggestion to those of you reading this book is to continue mimicking. If you would like, you can make crop circles in your bedroom with crystals. As an example, you can draw your own glyphs and hang them on your mirror so you see them frequently. You can put crop circles in your back yard. Or you can find another ET behavior that you would like to mimic — with the exception of abductions! You are drawn to mimic. Use your creativity and your imagination. See what you can come up with to begin mimicking the behavior in which you perceive ETs engage. You are going to see some interesting results.

In England there already are people building their own crop circles to look like the ones that appear in the fields. Is this part of what you are talking about?

Yes, it is. Whether they are consciously or unconsciously aware of it, it is their attempt at mimicry in order to bridge the gulf that lies between you.

Mimicry naturally occurs when two species confront each other. If you have two humans of different languages stranded on a desert island, you will use mimicry in order to build a common vocabulary with which you can communicate. It is only when the intellect starts getting in the way that you may resist your own initial impulse to mimic.

Last night I saw a red streak to the west, moving very quickly. Was I seeing a ship in that moment?

Yes. We would say it was a Zeta Reticuli ship.

Did they want to be seen?

Yes. Rest assured if they didn't want to be seen, they would not have been. They were, in a sense, responding to your willingness to see them.

The Zetas who were on the eastern hill, what prompted them to make the kind of contact they did as opposed to a more physical contact? I could clearly feel them even though I could not see them. If they can come that close and only allow their energy to be felt, what was the barrier?

First of all, we ETs who were involved in this experiment last night were running an experiment of our own. This experiment, from our point of view, was to give you the opportunity to see how receptive you are. So in a sense, we were your backdrop in order to test your own perceptive abilities. It was not meant to be an abductionfest last night! The Zetas, knowing this, allowed themselves to participate in the experiment with certain boundaries. This was not forced upon them. They recognized that ultimately your own perceptive abilities can benefit their interactions with you.

I was also hearing activity in the bushes. What was that?

We are aware of two things. There were some animals. Also, what you heard were part of the tests of your perceptive abilities. Yes, some of the noises were generated by your ET friends.

If it was generated, that does not necessarily mean someone was there.

Some of the noises were created by the physical presence of ETs, some of it was part of the perceptual tests.

Where were you when our experiment was taking place?

We knew someone would ask that question! I was in several places. I was in a Pleiadian ship that was in your vicinity. I was in the ship that landed. And at one point I was in the Association ship that was in the vicinity as well. But I was not walking your earth.

If you landed your ship, was there a purpose to the landing? Was it to see if we could perceive you?

Not so much to see if you would see us, because our estimation was that you would not consciously see us. It was more for you to feel the proximity of the energy of the ship being there. The closer we get to your Earth (such as in a landing), the more it grounds the idea of our presence for you. Symbolically, that is why we allowed the ship to land. Also, there was a respect on the part of the ships who were there, not to come in too close. If too many ships came in too close, your perceptual capacity would be overloaded.

Sasha, when I finished my regression today, I really felt like I had a release. I felt receptive to new information. Can you talk about that a little bit?

In the experience that all of you (without exception) had this weekend, you have allowed yourself to confront some of the obstacles to contact — most namely, your expectations and your fears. In confronting those internally, sitting with them overnight, and then having the regressions, you all allowed yourselves to release some of

173

the energy that you've held regarding the obstacles that have kept you moving at a slow pace. The release that you felt was very real. The importance of the release was not so much the actual memories that you reawakened; but rather the release itself was powerful.

In the chapter called "Releasing the Pressure" we talked about how important it is that this raw energy held within you is released. That stimulates integration within your consciousness, which will aid in your decompartmentalization and which will in turn allow you to be able to perceive more clearly and fully as well as retain a more solid memory of the experience.

Each and every one of you who participated in this research project will not ever be the same person. You may or may not notice the differences. Maybe down the road when you look back you will notice. But each of you have shifted very dramatically this weekend. The shifts that you've made will affect each of you as individuals but will also affect your mass consciousness. By the time this book is published, many of you will have shared your experiences with your friends. That will spread throughout the mass consciousness exponentially. By the time this material is read, individuals will be getting ideas about initiating their own contact programs. The doors that you have opened as individuals here will result in very powerful pathways cleared in the mass consciousness.

We would like to thank you for participating. For each of you had to confront portions of yourself in order to participate. This cannot help but change you.

I came away from the experience last evening feeling very beat up physically. I did not do anything particularly strenuous. Is that because of the proximity of the two visitors I was close to?

Each person will translate the energy they are exposed to in a different way. Let us say, first of all, that your belief system got a workout. Your body translated that workout in a way that reminded you and validated for you that the workout did in fact happen. That is one aspect of it. Another is that your proximity to the energies that you encountered accelerated you cellularly, so that your body was prompted to release stored energy and toxins at a faster rate than usual.

Any of you who are having physical symptoms of discomfort or

174

illness, it is absolutely without question connected to this experience. Either it is your resistance to this experience or your release into this experience. Perhaps a bit of both.

Does the idea of a ship landing have any connection to the concept of ascension?

Absolutely. Our definition of ascension is *integration*. Ascension *is* integration. Ascension is the movement from your physical, ego orientation "up" into the greater portion of yourself—your higher self. That is ascension—becoming one with your higher self.

As we have spoken about, the whole integration process is very tied in to preparing for contact. This is because as you integrate it means you decompartmentalize and become more of your greater self. The whole idea of ascension—meaning integration—is a process whose natural byproduct can be open contact.

In the greater sense of it, for all of you to meet a ship that lands and to have the experience in the best way you possibly can, you will need to be aligned with your higher self. Physically seeing ships clearly, without any filtering of your perceptions, is not necessarily something that can be maintained in your consciousness unless you achieve that alignment.

There are exceptions to this. We are talking in a general sense here.

In other words, is boarding a ship somehow equivalent to the ascension process?

Yes! Yes! Yes! Because very often the entities whom you meet (whether on the inner state or the physical state) are either your actual future selves, or their energy represents a future of your species. In order to connect with a future self of you, you will first need to confront the higher self, which then raises your vibration so that you can get to a common ground upon which to meet the future self. So [consciously] boarding a ship that has landed can be equivalent to an ascension process, because you must get to a higher level to do so.

We tested out the pendulum. How do you feel about our results? Are we using this to get definite answers, or to tap into information within ourselves?

175

The answers that were given to you by the pendulum, though they may be truth, are more importantly used to open doors within yourself. So first and foremost, think of the importance of those answers that you received in moving you in the direction you need to go. In retrospect, you will look back and see whether the answers are true. But there can never be definitive answers about the future. You all know that. Pendulums and other tools of divination read the most probable energy flows.

How much does the person with the pendulum affect the answers?

This is a very difficult question to answer, because it is different in each circumstance. Ultimately we are back to the idea that you create your own reality. This means that you as an individual and you as a group will co-create the answers you need to experience in order to move through what you need to move through. There is no difference between whether the pendulum reader is creating the answer or whether the answer is coming from the universe, because you are the universe anyway.

What does an ET experience when contacting humans?

Earlier in this book we have told you that when we come into your reality in ships, it is like a great sailing ship in a fog. Your mass consciousness, as we view it, is often like a fog. If we come across a conscious individual or group, it is as if the fog breaks and we can see a light below. The light to us represents conscious individuals placing themselves upon a common ground of equality with ETs. When we see you, it becomes obvious that our flow is to interact with you, and then we make contact.

What do the ETs feel?

Tremendous excitement that, in a sense, a group of people have awakened. In that wakefulness, there is a window for us to interact.

How do the ETs share this excitement among themselves? Do you say things, or make gestures?

It is mostly telepathic and telempathic. We will share the excitement in a way that is energetic rather than verbal. There is simply a group knowingness. It is very different from what you are used to in your reality. Our teams that are trained in this type of encounter can respond very quickly to your momentary wakefulness.

Let me give you the example of Janice again. She was sitting in her office and had a visitation by a Pleiadian. I described for you moment by moment what Janice was feeling. I will now attempt to describe for you what my Pleiadian colleague was feeling.

As my colleague materialized into the vicinity, there was a momentary sense of disorientation because of the density of your reality. We are also trained to adapt our vibrational frequencies, usually within three seconds, as we enter your environment. So my Pleiadian colleague, within those three seconds, adjusted her frequency to a comfort level within which she could interact. We cannot simulate your exact frequency because it is not compatible with our reality structure. So we are slightly more accelerated, but can still interface with your reality.

This Pleiadian being then walked into Janice's perceptual arena. As soon as Janice perceived the ET, there was a momentary distortion. This was because once Janice's attention was focused on the Pleiadian, there was a magnet (almost like a tractor beam) placed upon the ET that, if gone unchecked, could draw her further into your physical reality. The vibration of your physical reality feels to us very much like a black hole or gravity well.

Some ETs at this point have devices (if they are not trained mentally and energetically) that serve as shields to counteract this gravity-well effect. Normally the device or mental technique will throw up a shield around the ET and the beam put out from the human to the ET is reflected back to the human. Then the intense energy from the human comes back onto themself. This is one thing that causes humans to withdraw within themselves during contact.

Usually the ETs who are sent on physical missions will have extensive mental and spiritual training to isolate their own vibrations so that they do not succumb to the intense physical vibration of your reality. I am speaking mainly of Pleiadians and others of like vibration.

If, for instance, a Pleiadian being came into your reality who had none of the training or shields, he or she would experience a feeling of claustrophobia accompanied by pain in the cranial area. There is a sensation that humans often experience when they are about to faint. Their perceptions seem to be collapsing in on themselves. This is very similar to what the ET will experience. Nothing like this has happened to us in recent history. We are extrapolating from past experiences of our race. If the Pleiadian gets to a crisis point of losing touch with their own original reality, the human will actually serve as a center point for the ET. The human will automatically raise his vibrational frequency in response to the ET entering a crisis. This will maintain a homeostasis. Within the universe there is always balance. Every moment that you meet with an individual you are always compensating and keeping the balance.

What do the ETs talk about before and after a contact experience?

After an experience, all of our memories are catalogued in a holographic matrix. It is not a matter of us telling the story. Using my technology, we simply take one moment of time and place our hands upon a panel. In that singular moment my entire experience is transmitted holographically into what you would call a computer. That is how the experience is stored. Anyone who wishes to experience it can recall it.

Do you convey the experience to your friends?

Generally not. There is no need to. The people who are on the ship automatically, in one single moment of time, have access to that experience. If I am to converse about it (either verbally or telepathically), it is after they have experienced the holographic information.

So there is really no reason to have dialog as we understand it. They either knew it as it was happening or have access to it afterwards.

That is correct. Encoded within that holographic presentation are my own thoughts, feelings, and experiences, which they access as well in the entire matrix. I do not personally have to relay my experience.

So overall, you ETs don't have a lot to talk about, do you?

That is correct.

For all of us to suddenly have relationships to each other like you do would be rather shocking. It would be like a void for us.

That is correct. Even in your contact experiences now, many of you recall either being touched or viewed by an ET and having thoughts transmitted. That is, in a sense, the way your minds interpret the experience. It is much more of a fluid, simultaneous experience.

178

This really throws light onto how you relate to each other. It is 180 degrees opposite from us. There are difficulties in the contact experience. Implied in our relationships with everything there must be a back-and-forthness.

Yes. That is the nature of third-density polarized reality. Back and forth. However, all of our "conversation" is done simultaneously. There is no back and forth to it. Most of you have experienced momentary flashes of this type of communication.

To some degree we as ETs have to present to you the illusion of that back-and-forthness in order to give you a comfort zone of communication. But simultaneous to that illusion is the actual reality of simultaneous communication.

So we cannot initiate contact in terms of putting out a call and then waiting for your response. It is a simultaneous initiation.

You cannot initiate it unless we choose to play the game of polarity back and forth with each other.

So true contact is a simultaneous, spontaneous showing up of two or more parties.

Yes! That is the true nature of your universe. You live in a holographic universe, not a linear one. It is a necessary game, however. When you initiate contact, you must play the game of back-and-forthness because that game actually allows you to get to the point of simultaneity.

Are some ET groups steering clear of humans at this time?

Many of the groups who visit your planet recognize that groups of ETs are engaged in a formal contact program. Universal protocol often dictates that when that is occurring, though visitation and exploration is allowed, usually parallel contact programs are not encouraged. Usually.

But I assume that there are other groups who may or may not be part of the Association who are active in some small way.

That is correct.

I sense that during this weekend, there is a certain malleability. Everyone had a true, real experience, but it wasn't in a structure that I am used to.

179

Yes, and that is perfect because the whole contact experience is not in a structure that any of you are used to. Nor is it in a structure that any of you have been expecting. It will not adhere to how you have projected it to be.

At this time, we would like to thank all of you for participating. We wish to stress again that by the experiences you have had this weekend, you are helping to pave the road toward contact and toward the evolution of consciousness that many of you have been waiting for. Though you cannot yet see that what you are doing will result in contact, simply trust your inner knowingness and your feelings about it to point you in the direction of your continued awakening.

Everything you do to decompartmentalize yourself and to grow as a individual and spiritual being will aid in your preparing for contact. The metamorphosis of consciousness has already begun. You will simply open your eyes and begin to see it. Thank you for being pioneers. We *will* meet again . . . probably when you least expect it.

Δ Δ Δ

We have no conclusions to make from this research project based on the data alone. However, the information presented by Sasha, Bashar, and Germane in this book, combined with our research project, has reinforced several key ideas:

1. Humans are experiencing extraterrestrial and extradimensional contact and have been for quite some time.

2. The human mind fragments and represses these experiences in order to continue to provide us with an orderly view of reality.

3. On other levels of the human consciousness, we experience a constant processing of our contact experiences and it is just a matter of time until this understanding of the greater reality comes to the surface.

4. Humankind is preparing for a leap in evolution, which will be orchestrated by a change in our perceptions of reality. Our perceptions will change as we allow our consciousness to become more elastic. To do this, we must be willing to delve into the unknown.

5. Once our inner barriers have transformed themselves and our egos no longer fear contact with the unknown, human transformation awaits us on the horizon.

6. And finally, as we approach this horizon we will see beings, some like ourselves, who await our arrival with open arms. At last we will meet them on the common ground.

Now it is up to you, the reader, to decide your next steps. Choose wisely. If you wish to open contact with extraterrestrials, this means you must first be willing to go within and open contact with all aspects of yourself. For only in knowing yourself can you truly know another. And only in accepting yourself can you accept another fully in your reality. Then reality itself transforms.

If you are ready to participate in the next step of human evolution, begin *now*. For in this most important era of human history, you cannot wait for another to lead. Walk now into the dark and empty desert and trust in your destination. Remember that there is a canopy of stars above you. You are not alone. ∇

Epilogue

Sasha: In this book we've presented a lot of information about the human consciousness and how that consciousness responds to contact. We've also, to some degree, given you some information about how we as ETs perceive the contact experience in a broad sense from our point of view.

We've also suggested to you various things to do in your own personal growth that can help you to integrate and transform yourselves as individuals, which will then lead to the transformation of your society.

However, there is one other thing that we would like to stress. Probably one of the most significant things right now on your world that you can do — not only to prepare yourself for contact but also to prepare your world — is to take action.

Many of you upon your world have been waiting, wringing your hands, and looking forward to the day when your government is finally going to crack and reveal all the information that has been under wraps for decades. That day is not going to come the way you envision it. In fact, *that day will only come if you as a people and as individuals bring it about.*

So, of course, the most common question would then be, "Well, how do I as a singular individual bring about such a momentous event?" It is very important for you to begin acting as if we already exist. Begin changing your language and your thinking and your actions to reflect your surety in our existence. Because of this knowledge, allow your actions to begin to reflect outward into your world so that the passivity does not exist the way it used to. Act with certainty regarding our existence. Act as a People.

When you allow this knowingness to translate into action, you will assist in transforming the paradigm of thinking from one of "Unidentified Flying Objects in the sky" to one of extraterrestrial craft and their occupants. Allow yourselves to no longer reflect uncertainty. In your knowingness of our existence, begin to act as if we are already there. You will bring us further and more solidly into your reality by acting in this way.

You do not need your governments to validate our existence. In a sense, your government needs *you* to validate our existence. For it is only you, the People, in your actions and what you demonstrate to your world that will give confidence to your governments and your religious structures. It is then they will begin acknowledging and adapting to our presence. You have always heard that you, the People, are your government. Somewhere along the line you've allowed the government to validate reality for you. But remember, they are structures that *you* have created. Because of this, *you* must change them. They will not change independently of you. They will change *because* of you.

Allow yourselves to act in confidence, boldly becoming symbols of transformation. Be a comforting force for those rigid structures upon your world so that they will feel at ease in allowing themselves to open to this information. They look to you! They will open up, release information, and deal with this when you allow yourselves to be the ones calling the shots. So far, you've not been willing to do it.

In your mass consciousness we sense a growing urgency. You have all begun to understand the critical juncture that you've come to in your history. Upon your world there are so many difficulties ecologically, economically, and in the world population. As you are beginning to understand and recognize these difficulties and challenges, you must also balance this with the secrets and the fears that you've kept hidden within yourselves. The entire extraterrestrial phenomenon is one such secret. It has been a Pandora's box that you haven't been willing to open. Well, now it is time.

No one will lead you to the truth. You must be the leaders. It is you, and you alone, whose responsibility this is. Please know that you have all the tools necessary within yourselves to do this. But the one thing it will require is courage; courage combined with perseverance and a little bit of patience will allow you to achieve your goals. You must now start putting one foot in front of the other. Baby steps are quite all right. Keep moving. Allow yourselves to be the wayshowers. When you do this, all other aspects of your reality will follow.

The power for change lies within you. The power to orchestrate your own evolution lies within you. Are you ready to reach for the stars?

As you hold out your hands, your eyes searching the heavens for us, we will be there. It is time to create your future by opening your eyes, minds, and hearts *now*. We await your arrival. ∇

FREE CATALOG and INFORMATION

Thank you for your interest in Royal Priest Research. We would like to continue serving you. We offer a free catalog which lists our book titles and over 150 audio cassette tapes and transcripts derived from the work of Lyssa Royal.

If you would like to receive a free catalog, please send your name and address, along with two stamps, to:

Royal Priest Research

c/o P.O. Box 30973

Phoenix, Arizona   Postal Zone 85046

Once you communicate with us, you are automatically added to our mailing list. We respect your privacy and our list is never sold or given away. Your comments and letters are always appreciated. However, due to the large volume of mail received, personal responses are usually not possible.

Bookstores: Our books (*Preparing for Contact, Visitors from Within,* and *The Prism of Lyra*) are available from all major distributors including Atrium, New Leaf, Bookpeople, Baker & Taylor, Weiser, Moving Books, and Ingram.

Foreign Distribution: Our books are available through Gemcraft in Melbourne, Australia and Windrush Press in Gloucestershire, England. All other foreign inquiries should be made to Atrium Publishing Group at (707) 542-5400, or fax at (707) 542-5444.

Foreign Languages: *The Prism of Lyra* is available in the Japanese language within Japan from Neo-Delphi, Inc., the German language from Zweitausendeins (hard cover) and G. Reichel Verlag (soft cover), and in the Portuguese language throughout Brazil from Editora Roca. *Visitors from Within* is available in German from Zweitausendeins (hard cover) and G. Reichel Verlag (soft cover). *Preparing for Contact* is available in German through Zweitausendeins.

Source Material

CHAPTER 1: **Preparing for Contact.** From tape #133 *Preparing for Contact II*, March 5, 1993. Recorded in Berkeley, California. Questions provided by Keith Priest and public audience.

CHAPTER 2: **Exploring the Contact Experience.** Recorded in Scottsdale, Arizona. Part one is a private session for Larry Frank. Part two consists of questions from Keith Priest. October 14, 1992.

CHAPTER 3: **The Dream.** Recorded in Scottsdale, Arizona. October 15, 1992. Questions provided by Keith Priest.

CHAPTER 4: **Mechanics of First Contact - A Case Study.** Recorded in Scottsdale, Arizona. December 23, 1992. Questions provided by Keith Priest.

CHAPTER 5: **The Common Ground.** Recorded in Scottsdale, Arizona. January 11, 1993. Private session for Larry Frank with questions asked by Keith Priest.

CHAPTER 6: **Unconscious Resistance.** Recorded in Scottsdale, Arizona. January 20, 1993. Questions provided by Keith Priest.

CHAPTER 7: **Inside the Contact Experience.** Recorded in Berkeley, California. March 6, 1993. Excerpted from tape #134 *Contact Workshop*. Questions provided by Keith Priest and public audience.

CHAPTER 8: **Releasing the Pressure.** Recorded in Scottsdale, Arizona. March 31, 1993. Questions provided by Keith Priest

CHAPTER 9: **Beyond the Conscious.** Recorded in Phoenix, Arizona. October 6, 1993. Questions provided by Keith Priest.

CHAPTER 10: **Integration and Transformation.** Recorded in Las Vegas, Nevada at the 1993 International UFO Congress. December 1, 1993.

CHAPTER 11: **Finding Your Truths.** Recorded in Scottsdale, Arizona. March 31, 1993. Questions provided by Keith Priest

CHAPTER 12: **Designing Contact.** Recorded in Phoenix, Arizona. July 18, 1993. Questions provided by Larry Frank.

CHAPTER 13: Opening the Door to Contact. Recorded in Phoenix and Cave Creek, Arizona. November 20, 1993. Questions provided by Keith Priest and contact research group.

CHAPTER 14: Pieces of the Puzzle. Recorded in Phoenix, Arizona. November 21, 1993. Questions provided by research group.

EPILOGUE: Recorded on the road north of Kingman, Arizona. December 5, 1993.

About the Authors

Lyssa Royal holds a B.A. in psychology and is an internationally known channel, author, and lecturer from Arizona. She is the co-author of several books published in four countries including: *The Prism of Lyra: An Exploration of Human Galactic Heritage* (USA, Japanese, and German versions), *Visitors from Within* (USA and German versions), *Future Sex* (USA and Australian versions), and *The Sedona Vortex Guidebook.* She is featured regularly in publications such as *Connecting Link* and *The Sedona Journal of Emergence.* Lyssa channels and lectures around the world, conducts tour groups to sacred sites, and has appeared on national and international television and radio.

In 1979 Lyssa had a UFO sighting witnessed by her family that triggered a profound interest in the extraterrestrial phenomenon. After several more UFO sightings in the 1980s, Lyssa began a search for answers concerning Earth's connection with extraterrestrial civilizations. She diligently honed her channeling skills and began to receive information that has helped thousands worldwide in their quest toward understanding the ET enigma. Though she works quite often with extraterrestrial information, the practical application of what she channels is always of utmost priority to her.

Keith Priest is an independent researcher and author (*The Prism of Lyra* and *Visitors from Within*) living in Arizona. He studied music at Michigan State University, majoring in piano technology and historical tuning systems. Keith's life philosophy has always been to ask, "Why?" Through his research he has delved into ancient languages, biblical studies, anthropology, history, and religions, combining those studies with astronomy, mythology and psychology. Though he has never seen an extraterrestrial spacecraft (much less an extraterrestrial), his studies have shown him that the ET issue not only fits nicely into all these areas but in fact is an integral piece of the puzzle that may connect them all.

For a complete catalog from Royal Priest Research please write to: Royal Priest Research, c/o PO Box 30973, Phoenix, Arizona USA 85046.

INITIATING CONTACT

Explore the Contact Experience in the Andes of Peru with Lyssa Royal

December 3-14, 1995

For thousands of years the Andes has been an area of intense and repeated extraterrestrial activity. In December, Lyssa Royal will be facilitating group contact experiences at Machu Picchu, Peru, among other sites in the Andes. Many of the techniques that will be used for initiating contact are based on Lyssa's work in the book *Preparing for Contact.*

During the days the group will visit ancient Incan sites as well as participate in channeled sessions with Sasha (through Lyssa) which will prepare the group for the night time activities. During the evenings (weather permitting), the group will gather under the stars and practice Sasha's techniques for initiating extraterrestrial contact. Never before has Lyssa conducted an intensive of this length and depth in an area of the world known for its high level of ET activity.

If you would like more information and a complete itinerary for this unique adventure, please contact:

VISIONS TRAVEL & TOURS INC.

1-800-888-5509

THE PRISM OF LYRA

An Exploration of Human Galactic Heritage

by Lyssa Royal & Keith Priest

Available through your bookstore and through all major distributors.
ISBN: 0-9631320-0-8 Price: $11.95
Trade paperback, 113 pages

This is an introductory book which examines the idea of creation in a different light. In contrast to the notion that humans are the result of creation, it explores the idea that the collective humanoid consciousness (or soul) created our universe for specific purposes.

What are those purposes? Who is involved? These questions and many more are addressed, resulting in startling possibilities.

The Prism of Lyra then traces various developing off-planet races (such as the Pleiadians and Orions) through their own evolution and ties them into the evolving Earth. Highlighted is the realization of our galactic interconnectedness and our shared desire to return home.

Explore with us the passage through ...

THE PRISM OF LYRA!

"[This] research on the stellar teachings...is very accurate, complete, and meaningful...[This] information about their essence is the truth." —Barbara Hand Clow, author and editor at Bear & Co. Publishers

*The Prism of Lyra is available in the Japanese language and is distributed throughout Japan by Neo-Delphi, Inc.

Visitors from Within

by Lyssa Royal and Keith Priest

LYSSA ROYAL & KEITH PRIEST

Visitors from Within explores the extraterrestrial contact and abduction phenomenon in a unique and intriguing way. A combination of narrative, precisely-focused channeled material and firsthand accounts, this book challenges the reader to use the abduction phenomenon as a tool for personal and planetary evolution.

Visitors from Within will captivate you, move you, and encourage you to expand your beliefs about extraterrestrial contact ... forever.

"*Visitors from Within* is a great help in overcoming our fear of the unknown ... "
— Donald M. Ware, Eastern Region Director, MUFON

"...*Visitors from Within* makes a significant contribution to the way we think about the abduction experience... "
— Michael Lindemann, author of
UFOs and the Alien Presence: Six Viewpoints

"...The authors succeed in substantially extending the leading edge of research and reflection on this most troubling phenomenon. The transformational vision is both optimistic and breathtaking."
— Mark B. Woodhouse, Ph.D.,
Associate Professor, Georgia State University